T0278132

ROCK 'N' ROLL
RADIO
CONNECTICUT

MAGIC MOMENTS
& UNFORGETTABLE
DISC JOCKEYS

TONY RENZONI

Foreword by Dick Robinson

THE
History
PRESS

Published by The History Press
Charleston, SC
www.historypress.com

Copyright © 2025 by Anthony Renzoni
All rights reserved

First published 2025

Manufactured in the United States

ISBN 9781467157674

Library of Congress Control Number: 2024945300

Notice: The information in this book is true and complete to the best of our knowledge. It is offered without guarantee on the part of the author or The History Press. The author and The History Press disclaim all liability in connection with the use of this book.

All rights reserved. No part of this book may be reproduced or transmitted in any form whatsoever without prior written permission from the publisher except in the case of brief quotations embodied in critical articles and reviews.

ADVANCE PRAISE

In Tony Renzoni's new book Rock 'n' Roll Radio Connecticut: Magic Moments and Unforgettable Disc Jockeys, *Tony pays tribute to many popular disc jockeys and the Connecticut radio stations they worked for over the years. Many of these disc jockeys became locally famous and some have become true legends throughout the United States.*

Radio station disc jockeys are an integral part of the music process and have played an important role in the history of rock-and-roll. Along with live concerts, radio stations have served as a vital connection between the music and the listeners. Throughout the years, radio stations have exerted considerable influence on popular music whether it's rock, pop, rhythm and blues, soul or other music genres.

When the Young Rascals and the Rascals were ready to release their new recordings, radio listeners got to hear our recordings immediately. Radio on-air personalities played our songs and labeled our new recordings with terms such as "Hit to Be," "Hot New Single" or "Future Number 1." This helped raise the curiosity of their radio audience to listen to our music and attend our live concerts. Indeed, radio stations and their loyal fans were a contributing factor to the Rascals' success, with our thirteen Top 40 hits and three no. 1 recordings.

As I am a performing artist currently on tour, the radio disc jockey continues to be an important factor in our music journey. As I tour the country with my group, Felix Cavaliere's Rascals, disc jockeys across the United States have been instrumental in getting the word out about our concerts and our music, which we very much appreciate.

Whether it was with the Young Rascals, the Rascals, my solo career and now with my current group, Connecticut has certainly been an important part of my life. During the period of time that I lived in Connecticut, I recorded at least five albums and eleven singles with the Rascals before the group's breakup in 1972. Also while living in Danbury, I recorded and released at least four solo albums. In 1980, my solo recording "Only a Lonely Heart Sees" was a Top 20 hit in Connecticut, thanks to all the local radio stations and their wonderful fans.

I have found that there has always been a tremendous appreciation of music by Connecticut radio stations and music fans alike. Radio stations such as WDRC, WPOP and KC101 have been very supportive to music groups I have been a part of, both past and present.

Along with paying tribute to a number of Connecticut radio stations and many of their very popular disc jockeys, Tony shares recollections by a number of radio personalities—in their own words—as they reminisce about working in their radio stations. I find these recollections very fascinating, entertaining and of interest to readers. Tony also includes several in-depth (and interesting) interviews with on-air personalities.

Hall of Famer Felix Cavaliere in concert. *Courtesy of Warren Kurtz.*

I highly recommend Rock 'n' Roll Radio Connecticut: Magic Moments and Unforgettable Disc Jockeys, *along with Tony's previous outstanding rock 'n' roll books!*
—*Felix Cavaliere, Rock and Roll Hall of Fame inductee, Songwriters Hall of Fame inductee and member of the Rascals and Felix Cavaliere's Rascals*

⊙ ⊙ ⊙

Tony Renzoni's third Connecticut music book Rock 'n' Roll Radio Connecticut: Magic Moments and Unforgettable Disc Jockeys, *takes us back to our formative years immersed in radio and DJs.*

Remember waking up to a clock radio tuned to your favorite station and listening to a transistor on your way home from school? How about being the tenth caller with the correct answer to win a prize, hopefully a record by your favorite group versus listening to the worn-out tape of their hit song that you recorded off the radio?

Do you remember changing stations at certain times based on your favorite DJs' schedules? Were you lucky enough to meet radio DJs at events, and did they have wacky nicknames? How about the weekly countdowns to learn what songs were debuting at the bottom of the list and which song was the new no. 1 hit? Do you recall when you heard a local band's record get played and then calling your best friend to tune in? Then at night, did you try to broaden your listening range to distant cities to find out what they were playing? When you were old enough to drive with a carful of friends, did you hear someone in the car playing one of your favorite new songs on a transistor radio and then quickly change your car's radio station to find that song? Tony takes us back to those fun times, bringing nostalgic smiles to our faces.
Enjoy this latest exciting volume in Tony's series!
—*Warren Kurtz, contributing editor,* Goldmine, *the music collector's magazine*

⊙ ⊙ ⊙

Tony Renzoni has given us the definitive books about rock 'n' roll in Connecticut. With his book Connecticut Rock 'n' Roll: A History, *Tony paid tribute to the very talented music artists associated with Connecticut. Tony then wrote* Historic Connecticut Music Venues, *an homage to many of the landmark music venues in our state. Now, you can read about the many talented Connecticut radio disc jockeys in his new book* Rock 'n' Roll Connecticut: Magic Moments and Unforgettable Disc Jockeys. *It was these on-air personalities, past and present, that have brought so many wonderful songs to you through the magic of radio. Hear their stories and see their faces. Stay tuned, and don't touch that dial!*

—*Danny Lyons, WEBE 108 disc jockey*

⊙ ⊙ ⊙

The Alice Cooper group had built a great reputation. However, we knew radio was the key to mass success. Landing a record deal and recording an album meant nothing if people didn't know it existed. This is the importance and value of radio stations for both the recording artists and radio fans.

Whenever a radio station invited us to do something, we jumped at the chance. It was a pleasure, especially since radio personalities were fun to hang out with. Hearing your song on the radio is always a thrill. Tony Renzoni's new book Rock 'n' Roll Radio Connecticut:

Dennis Dunaway. *Copyright Philamonjaro.*

Magic Moments and Unforgettable Disc Jockeys, *demonstrates the impact that radio stations have had on rock-and-roll music throughout years. Tony's book also chronicles the careers and the fun and entertaining routines of many talented Connecticut radio personalities, including some who became legendary. I highly recommend this well-researched book to all music fans.*

—Dennis Dunaway, Hall of Fame artist and co-founder of the Alice Cooper group, the Flying Tigers and Blue Coupe

When I moved to New Haven from Detroit in 1970, I began working at radio station WAVZ. It was there that I got the true sense of competitiveness between radio stations in Connecticut and the highly dominant New York City stations and their radio personalities. And it was that exposure to competition coming from New York and the importance of the on-air personality and listener connection that prepared me for management during the evolution of rock on the radio.

I marveled at the competitive feel of Connecticut radio and the top station signals coming from New York. Connecticut broadcasters had their work cut out for them at a time when the medium and the music were evolving with the coming evolution of FM and the never-ending explosion of new and exciting music.

I was blessed to be in the right place at the right time when I was given the opportunity to join WPLR for its birth in 1971 and to be part of a team that brought new thinking to music radio programming. The quality of programming and intensity of competition of Connecticut radio was truly challenging and extremely stimulating.

It was a time to "break through" and bring the listener an experience that would both capture and inspire. It is fascinating to think back to a time when it was both risky and captivating to experiment with new approaches to listener involvement and entertainment. What we did and how we did it will always be the highlight of my professional life.

Tony Renzoni's book Rock 'n' Roll Radio Connecticut: Magic Moments and Unforgettable Disc Jockeys *captures both the professionalism, passion and enthusiasm for the radio art form during this vibrant era, and I'm thrilled to have been both a part of it and to read the stories of my competitors who were also my friends as well. This was a very special time driven by creative talent and thinking and you will now get a chance to experience how it all happened. I hope you enjoy reading about it as much as I enjoyed being involved in it.*

—Dick Kalt, former WPLR general manager

⊙ ⊙ ⊙

Christine Ohlman. *Photo by Irene Liebler and Sandy Connolly at Super9Studios.com.*

Tony Renzoni's previous twin books Connecticut Rock 'n' Roll: A History *and* Historic Connecticut Music Venues *have just gained a new and wonderful triplet.* Rock 'n' Roll Radio Connecticut: Magic Moments and Unforgettable Disc Jockeys, *celebrates the AM and FM radio stations and colorful on-air personalities who spread joy via the airwaves to every corner of the Nutmeg State and beyond. There's true music history here—lovingly told and tailor-made for great reading. Highly recommended!*

—Christine Ohlman, the "Beehive Queen," recording artist/songwriter

⊙ ⊙ ⊙

All five members of our original band were from Stamford, Connecticut. At the time we formed our band we began to play a lot in nearby New York City, especially in Greenwich Village. We soon built a large and very loyal fan base in New York City as well as the Stamford area.

In 1965, we started to get a little airplay on NYC's radio stations. At the same time, our local Stamford fans marched down to Stamford's radio station WSTC and pressured the station to play our new release "So Little Time." What we found amazing about that is the fact that WSTC had mainly a news and talk format. They were by no means a rock-and-roll station and would never broadcast the kind of rock music we played. But the station relented and played our song, thanks to our local Connecticut fans. Knowing the importance of radio airplay for

Ken Evans. *Courtesy of Ken Evans.*

rock bands like ours, we were grateful for this opportunity. Soon other radio stations in Connecticut and New York began to play our music. The year 1965 was also important to our band because that is when our group played on the hit TV music show Hullabaloo. Our appearance on that show gave our band national exposure.

Radio airplay has played a vital role in the introduction of our music to the station's listening audience. Bridgeport's WICC was really into our music early on and supported us greatly. In 1967, our song "Ding Dong! The Witch Is Dead" became the no. 11 song on Billboard's national music charts. The song reached no. 1 on Hartford's WDRC and was heavily played on all Connecticut radio stations.

The exposure our band received from radio stations and disc jockeys all across the country, including Connecticut, was enormous.

Tony Renzoni's book Rock 'n' Roll Radio Connecticut: Magic Moments and Unforgettable Disc Jockeys, *follows his previous successful rock-and-roll books* Connecticut Rock 'n' roll: A History *and* Historic Connecticut Music Venues: From the Coliseum to the Shaboo. *In this new book, Tony pays tribute to the many radio stations in Connecticut and their very talented on-air personalities. It features some of their zany but entertaining skits and routines, which have been a regular feature of many disc jockeys over the years.*

Tony's book Rock 'n' Roll Radio Connecticut: Magic Moments and Unforgettable Disc Jockeys *is a fun and very entertaining read.*

I highly recommend this book to all music fans everywhere.

—*Ken Evans of the Fifth Estate band*

This book is dedicated to all the talented on-air personalities and the radio stations they worked for throughout the years.

CONTENTS

CONTENTS

FOREWORD

It is an honor to write the foreword for this book about the many radio stations and on-air personalities that have graced Connecticut's airwaves throughout the years.

As an on-air broadcaster for over sixty years, I have worked with many radio disc jockeys throughout Connecticut and other parts of the country. Many of these radio disc jockeys have become lifelong friends.

In his new book *Rock 'n' Roll Radio Connecticut: Magic Moments and Unforgettable Disc Jockeys*, Tony Renzoni captures the true spirit and essence of life as an on-air personality. Moreover, Tony spotlights the fun and entertaining qualities of many of these disc jockeys.

As I look back, I have such fond memories of working at radio stations such as Hartford's WDRC. I arrived at DRC in 1964 just as the country first encountered the British Invasion and felt its profound impact on music history. Talk about being at the right place and at the right time. I was also a part of the friendly but fierce rivalry between WDRC and WPOP. Such fun that was!

I am pleased to say that I continue to be involved in on-air broadcasting. One of my recent ventures is hosting a two-hour program called *Dick Robinson's American Standards by the Sea*, which pays homage to music legends from the 1920s through the 1950s and is heard worldwide on great radio stations.

In his book, Tony pays tribute to many great on-air personalities that worked in a number of Connecticut radio stations. I know firsthand the talent and skills that these radio disc jockeys possessed. Many were charismatic figures with a perceptive instinct of what listeners wanted to hear. Indeed, some of them even became legends, remembered to this day for their zany but fun on-air routines and their uncanny ability to connect with their legions of fans.

Connecticut's contribution to the music scene has been significant and profound. The State of Connecticut has always had a tremendous appreciation of arts and entertainment. The people in this state really support the arts, including music of all genres. And the sudden emergence of rock and pop music was no exception. Residents of the state, especially teenagers, embraced the rock-and-roll phenomenon. Radio stations throughout the state provided teenagers the one vehicle they most needed—a format for them to listen to their favorite songs and, at times, hear from the artists themselves as on-air guests on these radio stations.

Music fans everywhere will enjoy reading this heartwarming tribute to the many talented artists known as radio disc jockeys.

For all of us who have a love of music and have been avid listeners of local radio stations throughout the years, *Rock 'n' Roll Radio Connecticut: Magic Moments and Unforgettable Disc Jockeys* is a must-read!

Dick Robinson
On-air radio personality and owner of radio stations
Founder/chairman of Connecticut Schools of Broadcasting since 1964
Currently CSB Media Arts Center
Founder/chairman of the nonprofit organization The Society for the
Preservation of the Great American Songbook

ACKNOWLEDGEMENTS

Colleen Renzoni, Dr. Kerry Renzoni, Sir Bronn, AJ, Al Anderson, Al Ferrante, Al Warren, Ashley Gee, Bill Koob, Bill Rienzi, Bill Stephens, Bob Paiva, Charles Rosenay, Chaz, Christine Ohlman, Danny Lyons, Dennis Dunaway, Dick Kalt, Dorothy Yutenkas, Fred and Emma Parris, Gary Shea, Ginny Arnell, Irene Liebler, Jack Camarda, Jeff Potter, Judith Fisher Freed, Kathy Barbino Mosgrove, Ken Evans, Ken Wolt, Marcia Win, Marty Ganter, Marty Morra, Mary Blacker, Mary Stone, Maureen Bradley, Mike Greene, Nick Balzano, Paul Pacelli, Paul Rosano, Paula Renzoni Crean, Philamonjaro, Sandy Connolly, Stan Nimiroski, Stefan Rybak, Steve Parker, Warren Kurtz and Gail Romanovich.

Thank you to the legendary Dick Robinson for writing the foreword to this book and also to Hall of Famer (and friend) Felix Cavaliere for all his support and advice. And a special thank-you to Ed Brouder for providing me permission to include portions of his wonderful WDRC/WPOP site.

Finally, I wish to thank my book publisher (Arcadia Publishing/The History Press) and, of course, editors Abigail Fleming and Mike Kinsella for all their wonderful guidance and support during this entire book process.

INTRODUCTION

Hey Anthony, turn on WDRC, they are going to play the song by that new group the Beatles. I heard it's great! All the radio stations are beginning to play this song." Thanks to my older brother Vince, this was my first introduction to a certain group from England that was about to take America by storm. It was also the first time I became aware of the effect that radio stations had on popular music to the mass audience.

Vince was my inspiration and resource person during the early days of rock 'n' roll. It was my brother Vince who introduced me to great songs by rock 'n' roll pioneers such as Elvis, Jerry Lee Lewis and the Everly Brothers. In terms of a pure rock 'n' roll song, it doesn't get too much better than "Don't Be Cruel" by Elvis Presley (with Elvis backed by the Jordanaires, Scotty Moore on lead guitar, Bill Black on double bass and D.J. Fontana on drums). Vince would come home with a bunch of great records for me to hear that he just purchased at Waterbury's Mattatuck Music Store. He also brought home the latest WWCO music survey from the store. What I always thought was cool (and I believe got me started on my rock 'n' roll journey) was the fact that Vince would first play Side A of the 45-rpm record on our record player, and then, much to my surprise, he would then flip the record over and have me listen to Side B. For example, he first had me listen to Jerry Lee's "Breathless" and then turned the record over and introduced me to Side B, "Down the Line" (almost equally as great as Side A). By doing this, I became familiar with songs that none of my classmates in Mt. Carmel Elementary's schoolyard had any knowledge of.

Thus began my interest and eventual immersion in the research of rock 'n' roll at a very early age. Thank you, Vince!

As instructed, I turned on my transistor radio to station WDRC, and the disc jockey described in detail the arrival of a group of "lads" from Liverpool, England. I thought to myself "Liverpool, where the heck is Liverpool, and what makes this group so special?" Keep in mind that rock bands were virtually nonexistent at the time. As if to answer my question, the disc jockey proceeded to explain that this group was causing quite a stir in Europe and was destined to become a sensation in the United States as well. He made the point of saying that some "experts" in England had already dismissed the group as a "passing fad." However, the DJ said that there is something unique about this group that is bound to elicit the same reaction from fans as Elvis did back in 1956. The DRC disc jockey predicted that this group was destined to be around for a long time (an accurate prediction). With that, the radio DJ played "I Want to Hold Your Hand" by the Beatles. Vince was right. That song, and its follow-up "She Loves You," were unlike anything I had heard before. And so, Connecticut's radio station WDRC (along with other local stations) was my introduction to the British Invasion artists and to songs by many, many more bands and solo artists after that. It was at this point that I became hooked on various radio stations and their talented radio disc jockeys.

How cool was it that music on local radio stations can be heard blasting at the beach, at picnics and just about everywhere else? Rock music even found its way in our church. As the parishioners began to file out of the church pews, the organist (Jerry, our grammar school classmate) would suddenly launch into a new song by the Rolling Stones that he had just heard on the radio the night before.

I vividly remember putting aside my high school homework, turning on my transistor radio and listening to one of my favorite disc jockeys announcing the radio station's Top 40 countdown or listening to the DJ's outrageous skits. After all, for teenagers back then, if it was a choice between homework or hearing your favorite disc jockey—you can guess which one won out.

Growing up, I became an avid listener to Connecticut radio stations such as WDRC, WPOP and my hometown radio station WWCO. I also checked in with some of the DJs at New York stations WABC and WINS. Like many other kids my age, I found that some of the on-air personalities on these radio stations became my favorite DJs, and I made a point of listening to them whenever possible. My favorite disc jockeys were the ones who were skillful in not only capturing my attention immediately but also had the

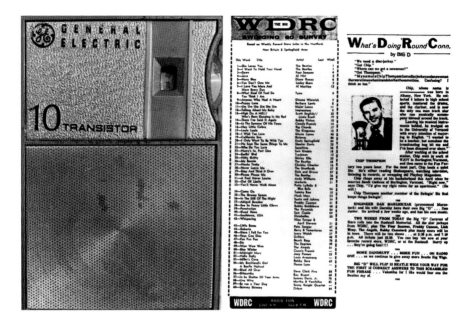

Left: My trusty transistor radio; *right*: WDRC music survey from February 17, 1964, with Beatles at no. 1 and no. 2. *Both author's collection.*

ability to hold my attention for long periods of time with their intriguing and entertaining routines. I, like many other listeners, caught on fairly quickly to their wacky skits, but we were still eager to follow along with these stunts right to the end. It was fun and entertaining. The really skillful on-air personalities made you tune in more to listen to their wild routines than listen to the music they were supposed to play. This, in at least my case, said a lot, since music was such an important part of my life. It still is.

These talented radio DJs made their weekly record countdown an entertaining experience and caused you to keep tuned in all the way until the no. 1 record was announced. I also remember the call-in contests where listeners would choose between two songs until the favorite of the final two was chosen as the no. 1 song. Not very scientific, but we didn't really care. The important thing was that we, the listeners, were part of the process of determining the most popular song during that given time, which may have differed from the more scientific record countdowns.

This book, *Rock 'n' Roll Connecticut: Magic Moments and Unforgettable Disc Jockeys*, is the third installment in my personal trilogy of rock 'n' roll books, the first two being *Connecticut Rock 'n' Roll: A History* and *Historic Connecticut Music Venues: From the Coliseum to the Shaboo*.

I thoroughly enjoyed speaking to many former and current on-air personalities during my lengthy research for this book. I learned how skillful and creative these radio personalities are and how, through a lot of hard work, they make what they do look so easy. I applaud them for entertaining all of us for so many years.

This book is intended to be read by the many, many fans of music heard from their favorite radio stations (or streaming online) and on-air personalities—not only here in Connecticut but everywhere as well.

I hope you enjoy *Rock 'n' Roll Connecticut: Magic Moments and Unforgettable Disc Jockeys* as much as I have throughout my many hours of research.

1

THE RADIO STATION DISC JOCKEY'S IMPACT ON POPULAR MUSIC

Disc jockeys are the connection between the music and their listeners and continue to be an important factor in the history of music

—*Felix Cavaliere*

Radio station disc jockeys' influence on popular music in our society cannot be overstated. The emergence of the radio disc jockey greatly contributed to the change in popular culture, specifically rock and pop music. All across the country, radio stations and their on-air personalities have had a profound and distinct effect on the music that their listeners wanted to hear. In turn, the success of recordings heard on radio stations greatly contributed to the success of recording artists.

Nowhere was this more evident than in the teenage culture, especially once rock and pop music became the dominant genres preferred by teenagers. Take, for instance, the weekly Top 40 Countdown by radio disc jockeys. Teenagers would tune in to their favorite radio station and listen intently as the songs played by the disc jockeys gradually moved through the Top 40, Top 20, Top 10 levels and finally to the no. 1 record for that particular week. At some point during the countdown, the disc jockey would usually introduce a "pick hit" record that the radio station believed would become a major hit. The more popular the song was on these countdowns, the greater the chances were of teenagers purchasing those records. Sometimes the on-air personalities would make these countdowns interactive with their audience, with the radio disc jockey pitting one song against another recording. The more colorful disc jockeys had their own unique way of getting listeners to actively participate in these contests. The listeners would call in to the radio station and cast their vote for which record they preferred. The winner of the final two songs remaining in the contest would be declared the no. 1 song of that local listening area. Although this was an unscientific way of determining a no. 1 record, these contests proved to be popular and fun for radio listeners, especially since the teenagers were an integral part of the process.

For many years, most radio music stations used a Top 40 format, listing the forty highest-ranking songs on the station's music chart. The term *Top 40* was developed, allegedly, when a radio pioneer observed that restaurant customers tended to play the same songs over and over on local jukeboxes—at the time, many jukeboxes held forty singles.

The radio station's music survey was a clever and unique way of getting the teenagers' attention on the most popular songs in the nation. Radio station music surveys were an important component in Top 40 music history. The one-page chart listings ranked the most popular songs based on a survey of local radio stations, retail sales and listener requests. The surveys showed the current ranked position of the songs along with their previous week's chart position. The radio stations would provide these one-page surveys to local record stores, which, in turn, handed out these surveys to their customers at no cost.

Each individual local radio station would have its own music survey. Thus the chart position of songs could vary somewhat from one radio station to another. For example, the ranking of songs on radio station WPOP in Hartford could differ a bit from radio station WWCO in Waterbury. The surveys were published weekly and designed to be distributed by local record stores to customers buying the latest 45 RPM records. The radio chart listings were issued from the late 1950s to the early 1980s. As album play on radio stations became popular, the music surveys would also include albums that were considered the most popular in the country. The peak period of music surveys was the late 1960s. *Billboard* magazine used radio station music surveys as one of the ways to compile its Top 100 singles charts.

Some surveys were simple in format and color, simply ranking the radio station's forty (or more) most popular songs for the current week. Other surveys were more detailed and a bit more colorful, showing the current ranking, the previous week's chart position, a photo of one of the radio station disc jockeys and radio station contests. The radio stations were able to advertise on the survey form. On-air radio personalities would inform and entertain listeners using the music surveys to count down the most popular songs in the listening area. The record stores used the surveys, in part, to entice customers to purchase more records than they initially had in mind. The customers liked the surveys because they were able to track their favorite songs and had a keen interest in finding out the no. 1 song on the chart listing. The recording artist would benefit, as customers purchased songs shown on the surveys, sometimes purchasing more records than they anticipated.

The rock music scene became a national phenomenon, emerging in every state across the country. And Connecticut was no exception. Indeed, the music scene in Connecticut was a microcosm of what was happening throughout the United States. Radio disc jockeys in Connecticut would conduct their Top 40 countdowns and have listener call-in countdown contests similar to radio stations in other parts of the country.

Likewise, the Connecticut radio stations released their own music surveys, which were popular, to listeners and record store customers throughout the state.

The following surveys pictured are examples of simple charts and more detailed surveys.

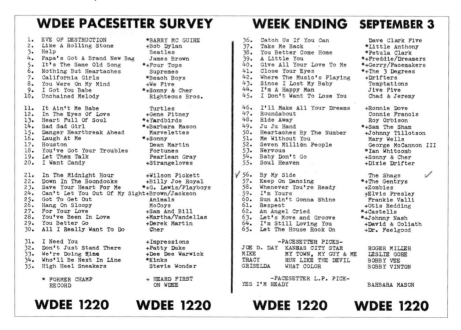

An example of a *simple* music chart survey. This survey merely shows the song's current ranking, the date of the survey and the call letters of the radio station. *Author's collection.*

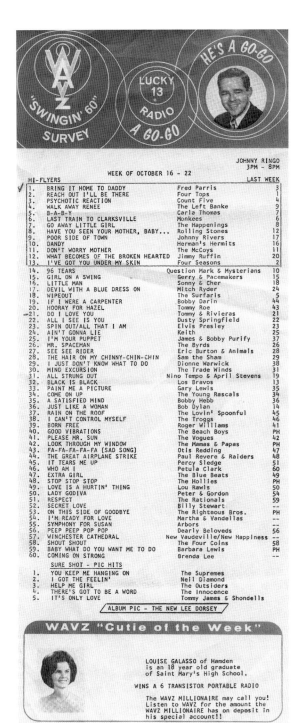

WAVZ "SWINGIN' 60" SURVEY • LUCKY 13 RADIO A GO-GO • HE'S A GO-GO

JOHNNY RINGO
3PM - 8PM

WEEK OF OCTOBER 16 - 22

HI-FLYERS			LAST WEEK
✓ 1.	BRING IT HOME TO DADDY	Fred Parris	3
2.	REACH OUT I'LL BE THERE	Four Tops	1
3.	PSYCHOTIC REACTION	Count Five	4
4.	WALK AWAY RENEE	The Left Banke	9
5.	B-A-B-Y	Carla Thomas	7
6.	LAST TRAIN TO CLARKSVILLE	Monkees	6
7.	GO AWAY LITTLE GIRL	The Happenings	8
8.	HAVE YOU SEEN YOUR MOTHER, BABY...	Rolling Stones	12
9.	POOR SIDE OF TOWN	Johnny Rivers	17
10.	DANDY	Herman's Hermits	16
11.	DON'T WORRY MOTHER	The McCoys	11
12.	WHAT BECOMES OF THE BROKEN HEARTED	Jimmy Ruffin	20
13.	I'VE GOT YOU UNDER MY SKIN	Four Seasons	2
14.	96 TEARS	Question Mark & Mysterians	10
15.	GIRL ON A SWING	Gerry & Pacemakers	15
16.	LITTLE MAN	Sonny & Cher	18
17.	DEVIL WITH A BLUE DRESS ON	Mitch Ryder	24
18.	WIPEOUT	The Surfaris	5
19.	IF I WERE A CARPENTER	Bobby Darin	44
20.	HOORAY FOR HAZEL	Tommy Roe	43
-21.	DO I LOVE YOU	Tommy & Rivieras	21
22.	ALL I SEE IS YOU	Dusty Springfield	22
23.	SPIN OUT/ALL THAT I AM	Elvis Presley	23
24.	AIN'T GONNA LIE	Keith	25
25.	I'M YOUR PUPPET	James & Bobby Purify	37
26.	MR. SPACEMAN	The Byrds	26
27.	SEE SEE RIDER	Eric Burton & Animals	28
28.	THE HAIR ON MY CHINNY-CHIN-CHIN	Sam the Sham	29
29.	I JUST DON'T KNOW WHAT TO DO	Dionne Warwick	38
30.	MIND EXCURSION	The Trade Winds	31
31.	ALL STRUNG OUT	Nino Tempo & April Stevens	19
32.	BLACK IS BLACK	Los Bravos	13
33.	PAINT ME A PICTURE	Gary Lewis	35
34.	COME ON UP	The Young Rascals	34
35.	A SATISFIED MIND	Bobby Hebb	36
36.	JUST LIKE A WOMAN	Bob Dylan	14
37.	RAIN ON THE ROOF	The Lovin' Spoonful	45
38.	I CAN'T CONTROL MYSELF	The Troggs	46
39.	BORN FREE	Roger Williams	41
40.	GOOD VIBRATIONS	The Beach Boys	PH
41.	PLEASE MR. SUN	The Vogues	42
42.	LOOK THROUGH MY WINDOW	The Mamas & Papas	PH
43.	FA-FA-FA-FA-FA (SAD SONG)	Otis Redding	47
44.	THE GREAT AIRPLANE STRIKE	Paul Revere & Raiders	48
45.	IT TEARS ME UP	Percy Sledge	51
46.	WHO AM I	Petula Clark	60
47.	EXTRA GIRL	The Blue Beats	49
48.	STOP STOP STOP	The Hollies	PH
49.	LOVE IS A HURTIN' THING	Lou Rawls	50
50.	LADY GODIVA	Peter & Gordon	54
51.	RESPECT	The Rationals	59
52.	SECRET LOVE	Billy Stewart	--
53.	ON THIS SIDE OF GOODBYE	The Righteous Bros.	PH
54.	I'M READY FOR LOVE	Martha & Vandellas	--
55.	SYMPHONY FOR SUSAN	Arbors	--
56.	PEEP PEEP POP POP	Dearly Beloveds	56
57.	WINCHESTER CATHEDRAL	New Vaudeville/New Happiness	--
58.	SHOUT SHOUT	The Four Coins	58
59.	BABY WHAT DO YOU WANT ME TO DO	Barbara Lewis	PH
60.	COMING ON STRONG	Brenda Lee	--

SURE SHOT - PIC HITS

1.	YOU KEEP ME HANGING ON	The Supremes
2.	I GOT THE FEELIN'	Neil Diamond
3.	HELP ME GIRL	The Outsiders
4.	THERE'S GOT TO BE A WORD	The Innocence
5.	IT'S ONLY LOVE	Tommy James & Shondells

ALBUM PIC - THE NEW LEE DORSEY

WAVZ "Cutie of the Week"

LOUISE GALASSO of Hamden
is an 18 year old graduate
of Saint Mary's High School.

WINS A 6 TRANSISTOR PORTABLE RADIO

The WAVZ MILLIONAIRE may call you!
Listen to WAVZ for the amount the
WAVZ MILLIONAIRE has on deposit in
his special account!!

A more detailed and more colorful survey showing current song ranking, song ranking for the previous week, station's call letters, station's logo, disc jockey photo, a weekly contest and a WAVZ Millionaire contest. Hamden's Louise Galasso was the lucky winner of a transistor radio. *Author's collection.*

Note: *Billboard* eventually began using a computerized method to determine its Hot 100 charts.

What Radio Listeners Have to Say in Response to This Question: What Has Been the Impact of Radio Stations and On-Air Disc Jockeys on Your Life?

The radio disc jockeys were my one link to being introduced to new songs, especially my favorites, including the Beatles, the Rolling Stones, the Beach Boys, Dusty Springfield and the Yardbirds. The on-air personalities on Hartford's WPOP and WDRC were exceptional. Radio personalities such as Dick Robinson, Joey Reynolds and Ken Griffin had a way of holding their listeners' attention throughout their wild but fun on-air skits and routines.

The disc jockey's impact on rock-and-roll music was enormous. The radio DJs across the country were an integral part of the success of rock music, especially in the 1960s. Each disc jockey had his own style, so professional and so much fun to listen to. Much of the time I listened to the Connecticut disc jockeys on my transistor radio. The character and sound of the transistor was unique, much like the vinyl record.

As an avid listener to WPOP and WDRC, I remember being glued to the radio stations to hear the weekly record countdowns. After hearing these great records on the radio for the first time, I made a point of purchasing many of these songs at local record stores such as Waterbury's Mattatuck Music Record Store and then play the songs over and over on my record player.

I have such fond memories of listening to these great Connecticut disc jockeys. I was a true fan, for sure!

—Marty Morra of The Villages, Florida, former Waterbury resident

My earliest radio memory was listening to WTIC's Bob Steele, mainly to hear school cancellations. The station was on every morning at our house, and I listened to all the artists of the early 1960s. It's where I first heard two of my all-time favorite songs, "The Girl From Ipanema" and "Theme from a Summer Place."

I was a big fan of WDRC and WPOP, especially Ken Griffin and Sandy Beach. I really enjoyed Ken's "Order of the Black Sox Club." My first band, the Insane, was booked through Ken Griffin's Christopher Productions along with our friends the Blue Beats.

Eventually, my favorite radio station was WHCN. Their wide range of musical styles was terrific to listen to. Wonderful musical diversity!

I was greatly affected and influenced by these great radio stations and on-air disc jockeys. Connecticut radio became such an integral part in the formation of my musical background!

—Gary Shea, member of Insane, New England and Alcatrazz bands

I grew up listening to Connecticut radio stations such as WPOP, WAVZ and WDRC. Actually, WPOP was my favorite station. I remember going to bed when I was about ten years old, putting my RCA transistor radio on the night table, listening to the radio station and then gradually drifting off to sleep.

Tuning into the crazy antics of the unpredictable and irreverent on-air personality Joey Reynolds was always a fun experience. I also made sure to follow the charismatic on-air disc jockeys Cousin Bruce (WABC) and Murray the K (WINS).

Another fond memory of mine was tuning into one of the Hartford radio stations (I believe it was DRC or POP) on Saturday mornings and afternoons. The station had a feature in which they pitted two of the Top 20 songs against each other. You had to call in and vote, and whichever song won, they would keep playing it. One morning, "California Girls" won something like nineteen times in a row. That's all they played until the Stones' "Satisfaction" knocked it off. It was so much fun.

They were all such great stations with entertaining and influential on-air radio personalities that had a major effect on many listeners, including myself!

—Paul Rosano, musician

Being a teenager during the '50s and '60s, AM radio was our connection to the music world. Tuning in late nights, early mornings or in between, we would be entertained and have a chance to listen to our favorite records. Some of the local radio stations out of Connecticut that I listened to

constantly were WAVZ, WDRC, WPOP, WTIC and WICC. All these stations provided so many special memories. The late radio DJ Al Warren of WICC was a friend and supporter of our band the Sultans. Thank you AM radio and all the amazing radio disc jockeys for spreading the sound of music through the airwaves.

—Nick Balzano, former member of the Sultans band

Growing up in Connecticut, I was an avid listener of local radio stations such as WDRC and the stations' great on-air radio disc jockeys. The music they played was second to none.

Whenever I came home from school or had time during the weekends, I would tune in to these local radio stations to hear music or delight in the wonderful antics of their on-air personalities.

Every time I got together with friends, we would all spontaneously sing and dance along with the great music played on these stations.

I cannot imagine my life without music that was played on local radio. I have such joyful memories of Connecticut radio stations and all their very entertaining on-air radio disc jockeys!

—Maureen Bradley of Scottsdale, Arizona, former Connecticut resident

2

SOCK HOPS AND RECORD HOPS HOSTED BY RADIO PERSONALITIES

From Sock Hops to Record Hops

In the mid-1940s, local radio disc jockeys began hosting sock hops throughout the United States. Teenagers would congregate in local gymnasiums and dance halls to listen and dance to the music of popular recording artists of that era, such as Frank Sinatra. For the most part, the music that the teenagers would dance to was played on vinyl records.

In an effort to protect the varnished floor of the gymnasium, teenagers were required to remove their shoes and dance in their socks, thus *sock hop*. The term *bobby soxer* grew out of the popularity of these sock hops, referring to teenage girls who would dance in their bobby socks because of the no-shoes requirement when dancing in gymnasiums. The bobby soxer was celebrated in hit songs such as Chuck Berry's "Go, Bobby Soxer" and Frankie Avalon's "Bobby Sox to Stockings." The term was also popularized in movies like *The Bachelor and the Bobby-Soxer* starring Cary Grant and Shirley Temple.

As music venues expanded to outdoor events and local clubs, the sock hop was replaced by the record hop. Disc jockeys of local radio stations such as WPOP, WICC and WDRC began hosting record hops and sometimes would introduce local bands and solo recording artists who performed live at these events.

WDRC's popular disc jockey Dick Robinson hosted many local record hops. Jim Gallant and other hosts of the popular *Connecticut Bandstand* TV

A 1951 Alan Freed record hop. Alan Freed broke down racial barriers with his record hops and concerts. *Courtesy of Judith Fraser Freed.*

dance show played host to many record hops throughout Connecticut. Also, famed disc jockey Alan Freed hosted record hop contests on his *Big Beat* TV show. Bridgeport's WICC radio station promoted record hops on June 12, 1959; June 19,1959; and July 6, 1961. In addition, Harry Downie at Bridgeport's Barnum Festival Midway hosted hops in Pleasure Beach park. Downie's record hops featured local recording artists such as Cookie and Charley, who were fan favorites on the *Connecticut Bandstand* dance show. The duo had a popular local hit recording, "Let's Go Rock and Roll."

National and local recording artists benefited from the exposure of their songs played by disc jockeys during these sock hops and record hops.

Whether these events were called sock hops or record hops, local disc jockeys hosted them as a way for teenagers to gather in one place and just have a fun experience.

RECORD HOP
AND SHOW
Saturday - Nov. 8th
City Hall Aud.
8 to 11 p.m.
in person
JIM GALLANT

**Star of WNHC-TV Bandstand
Show — Plus the Fabulous
"Teenrockers"—"Premiers"
"Del - Terriers," and special
guests, "Little Anthony" and
"The Imeprials."**

Left: Connecticut disc jockey Jim Gallant hosted area record hops along with his popular TV show *Connecticut Bandstand*. *Author's collection*.

Below: A 1957 record hop contest on Alan Freed's *Big Beat* TV show. *Courtesy of Judith Fraser Freed*.

Record Hops Hosted by Disc Jockey Jim Gallant

Prior to going on stage for one of Jim Gallant's Lake Compounce shows in Bristol, Connecticut, the Premiers were in the dressing room practicing for the song "I Wonder Why." All of a sudden, the door opened and in walked four guys who stood there and watched us finish the song. One guy stepped forward and asked, "Are you guys planning on singing that song tonight?" My brother Roger Koob replied, "Yeah, why?" The other guy responded, "Well, that's our song." At first, we didn't recognize any of these guys. But it was Dion who asked the question. So, we all had a good laugh. The following Sunday, while the Premiers were walking up Broadway in NYC, we ran smack into the Belmonts. All the group members stopped, and we had a really nice conversation about music.

—Bill Koob of the Premiers

Connecticut Bandstand

Connecticut Bandstand's popular disc jockey Jim Gallant hosted numerous record hops at Bristol's Lake Compounce. The record hops were known as the *Jim Gallant Lake Compounce Shows.* In 1957, Gallant introduced the Lake Compounce record hops, which were initially held on Thursday nights. To attract more high school students, the record hops were moved to Friday nights (8:00 p.m. to 11:00 p.m.) beginning on May 15, 1958. Gallant also hosted many record hops in other areas of Connecticut.

Gallant's record hop shows were popular with teens and featured some well-known guest recording artists, including Bobby Rydell performing "Kissing Time," Dion and the Belmonts, Johnny Tillotson and others. Also featured were regional and local group favorites (such as the Premiers) and regulars from Jim Gallant's *Connecticut Bandstand* TV show.

3

MUSIC CONCERTS SPONSORED BY CONNECTICUT RADIO STATIONS

In the old days, we didn't have internet, Facebook, Instagram or any other social media—but we did have our music. And it was music that bonded us together

—*Felix Cavaliere*

Because my dad (Charlie Parker) was a programmer at WDRC, I spent most of my early years backstage with my father at all the WDRC/Big D shows. As a teenager I worked for a couple of years with Jimmy Koplick (a good friend) at Dillon Stadium. Some of the wildest and biggest rock acts I have ever seen! I am so blessed because, as Charlie's son, I got to personally meet famous performers such as Jimi Hendrix, Janis Joplin, the Four Seasons, the Beach Boys, the Rolling Stones, Bobby Rydell, the Supremes, Elton John and many more.

I loved all the rock concerts at Connecticut music venues!

—*Steve Parker, WTIC on-air personality*

Connecticut radio stations hosted numerous music concerts in the state. The following are a small sample:

THE GENE PITNEY SHOW, hosted by Hartford's WPOP
WPOP hosted a Gene Pitney show in August 1967 at the Bushnell Memorial in Hartford, Connecticut. The performing acts in the Gene Pitney show (in

Left: Gene Pitney show tour poster; *right*: group photo of artists on tour with the Gene Pitney show, 1967. *Both courtesy of Ken Evans, of the Fifth Estate band*

order of appearance) were Ronnie James Dio and the Prophets (opening act), the Music Explosion, the Fifth Estate, the Buckinghams, the Easybeats and the Happenings. Rockville's legendary Gene Pitney closed out the show with an impressive performance.

THE ROLLING STONES CONCERT hosted by Radio Station WPOP
WPOP radio sponsored the Rolling Stones' performance at Dillon Stadium on June 27, 1966.

Music Concerts Hosted by WDRC

WDRC hosted music concerts at Hartford's Bushnell Memorial and other music venues, including:

April 22, 1965	Gene Pitney
January 30, 1966	Four Seasons, Mitch Ryder and the Detroit Wheels
November 20, 1967	Beach Boys, Buffalo Springfield
March 22, 1968	Jimi Hendrix
May 18, 1968	The (Young) Rascals
September 25, 1970	Led Zeppelin, Eric Clapton, Stephen Stills and others
July 10, 1972	Rod Stewart
August 4, 1972	Alice Cooper
September 13, 1978	Bruce Springsteen

Left: Brian Jones (*left*) and Mick Jagger backstage at Dillon Stadium (June 1966). The Stones concert was coordinated by Bob Paiva, WPOP promotions director. *Courtesy of Bob Paiva.*

Right: Bob DeCarlo. *Courtesy of Ed Brouder.*

Battle of the Bands TV Special

WDRC's Bob DeCarlo and WPOP's Billy Love hosted the *Battle of the Bands* TV special on Connecticut TV Channel 30 on August 11, 1970.

4

WDRC-AM

WDRC Background

WDRC-AM (1360) was first licensed to air as far back as 1922 and was the first radio station in Connecticut. In the beginning, the station's call letters were WPAJ. The call letters were changed on February 21, 1925, to WDRC (Doolittle Radio Corporation, a tribute to then owner Franklin Malcom Doolittle). The station was also known as DRC.

WDRC eventually became a Top 40 radio station.

In the 1960s and 1970s, there was a major rivalry between WDRC and WPOP 1410, both located in Hartford, Connecticut. The competition for younger listeners was especially fierce. In 1975, the battle came to an abrupt end when WPOP dropped pop/rock music and switched to an all-news format.

Like WPOP, WDRC switched to an all-news format in the 1990s.

Notable Radio Personalities

Charlie Parker

Charlie Parker was, as far as I am concerned, the god of all program directors, past, present or future.

—Robert Abbett (aka Rabbett), disc jockey

Charlie Roy Parker was born in Hartford on March 1, 1925. His career at WDRC began at age seventeen. On one occasion, the DRC secretary, Anne Welch, was asked to give Charlie a tour of the station. Anne, who was better known as "Patty" Welch, worked as clerical staff at Hartford's Pratt & Whitney before joining WDRC. On rare occasions, Anne appeared on-air at DRC. She became known on-air as Patty, a name she earned because her ready sense of humor meant she often giggled. A fellow staff member called her a Silly Patty, and the nickname stuck.

Patty and Charlie began dating, and on October 20, 1945, they became husband and wife.

Without question, Charlie Parker was the brains behind WDRC's success for many years. As program director and later vice president of programming, Parker had a keen ear for hit music and was a talented writer. Charlie, along with music director Bertha Porter, had an uncanny knack of predicting songs that would become national hit records. In 1975, *Billboard* magazine named Charlie Parker the Program Director of the Year.

Charlie's genius at spotting trends allowed WDRC to capitalize on the many crazes of the day, including the British Invasion. Charlie also voiced many station promos and special features, and he was responsible for WDRC's distinctive sound.

Charlie was a superb motivator of talent, and many broadcasters credit Charlie Parker for their successful radio careers. Charlie Parker was sixty-eight when he passed away on March 14, 1993.

Praise for Charlie Parker

Charlie Parker told me three things that I will always remember. First, Always surround yourself with good people (they can make or break you); Second, Don't be afraid to share the credit with them; Third, Always try to hear your radio station the way a listener would (not as a jock or program director).
—Jack Lawrence, former WDRC disc jockey

Be aware of your different audiences—the factory people, the hamburger stands, the nurses, the party animals, people who stay up late and those who get up really early and *make the flow invisible.*
—Advice from Charlie Parker given to WDRC disc jockey Robert Abbett
(better known as Rabbett)

Above: Charlie with his son Steve (far *right*). *Courtesy of Ed Brouder.*

Opposite: Charlie Parker, WDRC program director. *Courtesy of Ed Brouder.*

Charlie Parker was ahead of his time in many, many respects. He was the single most innovative programmer I've ever known. I had enormous respect for that man as, I believe, all who worked for him did.
　　　　　　　　　　　—Jim Nettleton, WDRC on-air personality

Bertha Porter

Bertha Porter made my career.
　　　　　　　　　—Big Al Anderson, Wildweeds, NRBQ, solo artist

While seldom heard on the air, the influence of Bertha G. Porter was widely felt off the air at WDRC for almost a quarter of a century.

Born in Springfield, Massachusetts on July 24, 1915, Bertha joined WDRC on June 4, 1945, helping out with bookkeeping and on the telephone switchboard. At the time, local radio stations didn't play a great deal of recorded music. But Bertha was put in charge of WDRC's collection of thirty thousand records. As record librarian and later music director, Bertha was tuned in to the tastes of contemporary America.

Although she didn't look the part, Bertha easily segued from easy listening music to rock 'n' roll—so much so that she was credited with having an extremely high rate of accurately predicting records that would become national Top 100 hits and even some that would eventually reach the Top 10 on the national record charts.

For years, one of Bertha's important chores every Thursday was telephoning three dozen Connecticut record retailers to collect the sales data she depended on to formulate the Big D Swinging Sixty Music Survey. Radio stations would use record sales along with such things as customer requests to develop their radio station music surveys.

As previously noted, most radio music stations used a Top 40 format,

WDRC's Bertha Porter, 1964. *Courtesy of Ed Brouder.*

listing the forty highest-ranking songs on the station's music chart (WDRC music surveys usually listed the their top 60 songs). Radio station music surveys were an important component in Top 40 music history.

Bertha's philosophy for picking new records was simple:

> *Either I like the record or I don't. But I'm not so stubborn that if a record becomes a hit anyway I'll ignore it. There have been records that I didn't like that became hits…but before they did, we were playing them.*

WDRC program director Charlie Parker praised Bertha's work ethic:

> *She planned out every announcer's show.….She wrote it out on a yellow legal pad. Every day she would plot out every show—how many male vocalists, how many females, how many instrumentals; nothing got played at WDRC unless Bertha Porter said so.*

Hartford and Cleveland were secondary markets with reputations for being good places to test new record products, so a few minutes with Bertha was a coveted prize for promoters from labels large and small. Her choices of music resulted in national recognition and at least fifteen gold records for being the first to play singles that went on to become national hits. Among the awards she received were the following:

Summer 1963	Gold record for Al Martino's "I Love You Because"
January 1964	Winner of the 1963 Music Director of the Year award from trade magazine the *Gavin Report*
January 1966	Winner of Music Director of the Year from the *Gavin Report*
March 1966	Gold Record (no. 5) for the Wonder Who's "Don't Think Twice"
October 1966	Gold Record (no. 6) for "See You in September" by the Happenings
1966 and 1967	Winner of Music Director of the Year from the *Gavin Report*
January 1967	Gold Record (no. 7)

While the on-air personalities received most of the attention and recognition, those same radio disc jockeys knew full well how important Bertha was to WDRC and to their careers.

Bertha had an uncanny knack of choosing records that would appeal to DRC's teenage listeners. Big Al Anderson (Wildweeds, NRBQ) discovered this for himself. Charlie's son Steve recalled how Bertha brilliantly predicted Al's first hit song, which she insisted that the disc jockeys play on WDRC:

> *I remember when Al Anderson used to hang around the WDRC radio station and hope that we could play some of his music that he wrote and recorded. Our WDRC music librarian Bertha Porter heard "Ain't No Good to Cry" and told Al, "That's your hit!" To this day, Al always gives Bertha credit as the one who got him started and gave him his break as a recording artist. When I see Al, he would always remind me that "Bertha Porter made my career!"*

Former WDRC production director Dave Overson tells the story of when the song "Sherry" by Frankie Valli and the Four Seasons was turned down by station after station. However, when Bertha Porter first heard the song, she told Charlie Parker, "This is a hit record!" Charlie agreed, and WDRC began playing the song consistently. Frankie Valli later confirmed this, and when asked, Frankie replied, "Charlie Parker and Bertha Porter are both responsible for establishing the Four Seasons' career by believing in our song and by believing in me. I owe them both a great debt of gratitude." On Friday, November 20, 1992, WDRC FM staged its tenth annual Legends of Rock and Roll concert at the Hartford Civic Center, preceded by an invitation-only reception in the atrium of the Goodwin Hotel. Charlie Parker and his family were greeted as VIP guests. During the concert, rock 'n' roll Hall of Famer Frankie Valli interrupted the Four Seasons' performance. He called Charlie up on to the stage to publicly thank him for all WDRC had done to support the Four Seasons during the previous three decades.

At the time of Bertha's resignation from WDRC in 1969, *Cash Box* magazine noted that she was "one of the most influential people in rock radio programing." The last thing Bertha did prior to leaving WDRC was add "Honky Tonk Women" by the Rolling Stones as a "Hit-To-Be." Talk about going out a winner!

5

WDRC RADIO DISC JOCKEYS

Dick Robinson

If Charlie Parker was the heart of WDRC, Dick Robinson was the soul.
—WDRC site

Nicholas "Dick" Robinson was born on April 17, 1938, in Malden, Massachusetts. He attended Malden High School (class of 1956) and was heavily involved in drama. He spent the summer in Maine with a stock theater company, appearing with Anne Baxter and Tyrone Power in *John Brown's Body*. While still in high school, Dick hosted many record hops. He then attended the Leland Powers School of Radio, Television and Theater in Boston and soon became an on-air announcer at radio station WARE in Ware, Massachusetts. At WARE, he played records, read newscasts, sold commercials and eventually received promotion to program director. After WARE, Dick worked at radio stations in Holyoke and Springfield, Massachusetts, and Providence, Rhode Island.

In 1964, Dick joined the on-air staff at Hartford's WDRC, where his 8:00 p.m. to 1:00 a.m. shift became known as the "Dick Robinson Company" or "DRC on DRC." His nighttime ratings were in double digits, and Dick became embroiled in a fierce competition for ratings with cross-town rival Ken Griffin at WPOP. One of his radio skits was the "Big D Late Late Show," which featured take-offs on show business celebrities appearing in mythical movies on Channel 1360. WDRC engineer Bob Cole appeared from time to time as man-on-the-street reporter "Humble Harvey Humble." Dick's routines also involved a number of Lone Ranger and Tonto jokes, and he regularly greeted his call-in listeners with Tonto's trademark "Hey Kemosabe." One of Dick's strengths was sounding like a friend to legions of teenagers who tuned in every night. Much of his show involved telephone interaction with listeners.

Dick Robinson, WDRC. *Courtesy of Robinson Entertainment, LLC.*

Dick founded the Connecticut School of Broadcasting (CSB) in September 1964. Numerous WDRC colleagues served as assistant directors of CSB, including Bill Hennessey, Bob Ellsworth, Jim Jeffrey and Walt Pinto (aka "Kent Clark"). Robinson is responsible for hundreds—maybe thousands— of broadcast careers as the founder of CSB.

November 1964 saw the release of the novelty 45-rpm record "Beatnik DJ" by Dick Robinson and the Nite Niks. The song was released on Connecticut's FUN record label and became Robinson's theme song. "Beatnik DJ" appeared on WDRC's radio station survey for three weeks in 1964, peaking at no. 52. The Nite Niks were actually the group Tommy Dae and the High Tensions. The record's Side B was "Give Me Love" by Tommy Dae and The Nite Niks. Singer-songwriter Tommy Dae (born Frank Draus Jr.) hailed from the Rockville/Vernon area of Connecticut and performed in a variety of music genres, including rock, pop, ballads, garage rock, novelty, country and psych rock. Dae recorded with his groups the High Tensions (a.k.a. the Tensions), the Tensionettes and the Nite Niks. The Tensionettes consisted of Annette Lettendre and Linda Draus (Tommy's sister). Robinson released another novelty tune on Connecticut's FUN label the following year (October 1965) called "Fraze Kraze" (a.k.a. Fraze Craze), after a popular phone-in feature on his show. Side B was a tune by the Tensionettes called "He's The Boy I Love."

In January 1965, Dick began hosting his weekly "Saturday Night House Party," and in April he instituted a nightly "Big D Shindig" from 8:00 p.m. to 9:00 p.m., keying on the popular ABC-TV *Shindig* show. Even though he was on the air six nights a week, Dick hosted hundreds of record hops. It was not unusual for Dick to host several record hops on a given Friday night. This prompted WDRC's Sandy Beach to jokingly announce on-air, "There will be a cut-out of Dick Robinson at Windsor Locks High school's record hop tonight."

Robinson managed to meet the Beatles and was involved in one of their press conferences. When Dick interviewed the Rolling Stones at the WDRC studio, the Stones nearly caused a riot as a swarm of teenagers greeted them that afternoon. Robinson reflected on joining WDRC at the time of the British Invasion:

> *I was in the right place, on the right job, at the right time. We were in the break-out area for new record releases, and we released them all, even if we had to pick the records up at Kennedy International Airport when the latest Rolling Stones' and Beatles' hits arrived by overseas jet.*

The year 1967 brought several changes to WDRC and Dick Robinson. DRC had already successfully raided WPOP and installed its nighttime host, Ken Griffin, in Dick's old slot. The legendary Joey Reynolds began a new early-evening shift, and Dick settled in the afternoon drive shift.

By 1968, Dick was only on the air Saturday afternoons and Sunday evenings. In November 1969, he was named WDRC's sales manager. And in mid-1974, Dick was appointed vice president and station manager of WDRC.

Left: Dick Robinson (WDRC DJ) involved in a Beatles press conference, 1965; *right*: Dick Robinson interviewing the Rolling Stones (at the WDRC studio) prior to their performance in Hartford. *Both courtesy of Robinson Entertainment, LLC.*

Left: Dick Robinson with Cher, 1965; *right*: Dick Robinson in the WDRC dune buggy. *Both courtesy of Robinson Entertainment, LLC.*

Robinson resigned from WDRC in February 1976, and in the following year (April 1977), he became a partner in the purchase of Farmington's radio station WRCH AM/FM.

On January 9, 2000, he launched a new show *Dick Robinson's American Standards by the Sea*, live from the Robinson Media Group's motor yacht named *Airwaves*, which is docked at different ports from Maine to the Bahamas throughout the year. The program can be heard on station WJMJ (Prospect, Connecticut), Saturdays from 6:00 p.m. to 8:00 p.m. and Sundays 10:00 p.m. to midnight.

Dick Robinson's on-air career path is one that few in the radio industry have equaled.

Notable WDRC On-Air Radio Personalities

Joey Reynolds

The original shock jock, Joey Reynolds is one of radio's best known and most colorful personalities.

—*WDRC/WPOP site*

Considered by many to be the original shock jock, Joey Reynolds came to Hartford's WDRC after stints in eleven other radio stations. Joey was extremely popular in his hometown of Buffalo, New York, at radio station WKBW. However, like many other radio stations, management felt a need to let him go because of his outrageous antics.

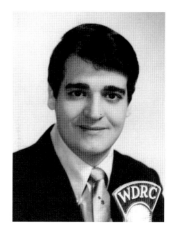

Joey's introduction to Hartford was at radio station WPOP, where he introduced Connecticut listeners to his "Royal Order of the Night People."

Reynolds started at WDRC the night after Christmas in 1966. He was sandwiched between Dick Robinson and Ken Griffin, working the 6:00 p.m. to 9:00 p.m. shift. Joey captivated his listeners with his energetic and entertaining style. He was largely undisciplined on-air, frequently straying from the format to go off on a tangent in his well-known

Joey Reynolds. *Courtesy of Ed Brouder.*

stream-of-consciousness monologues, which his legions of fans loved. Joey's characters included "Captain Pumpernick," the "Crooked Cop" and "Jack Armstrong, the All-American Weather Boy."

Joey stayed at DRC until the spring of 1968, when he was let go due to his wacky antics and a controversial statement about Hartford's mayor. Reynolds reappeared at WDRC in September 1969, but only to fill in during Ken Griffin's two-week vacation. He then moved on to numerous other radio stations. All told, Joey worked as an on-air personality for over twenty-five radio stations, having been fired by some.

While his time as a radio disc jockey in Connecticut was relatively short, Joey Reynolds is one of the most fondly remembered on-air personalities in Connecticut's radio history.

Ken Griffin

Joseph T. Mulhall Jr. was born on June 29, 1937, in Waterbury, Connecticut. Using his persona Ken Griffin, he worked at several radio stations in his hometown, including WBRY, WATR and WWCO. A favorite with teenagers, Ken became well-known throughout the region, including the Hartford/Springfield market. While at Hartford's WPOP, he hosted a weekly TV show on Channel 18 in Hartford.

Ken Griffin did character voices, and a major part of his show was a married couple, "Fats Phontoon" and her husband, "Rocky Hill." Ken would hold a three-way conversation with himself, Fats and Rocky that was so well done that the audience really believed Fats and Rocky were separate people. WPOP assistant program director Bob Paiva recalled Ken's routine:

Ken Griffin. *Courtesy of Ed Brouder.*

> *I remember well that on "Fats" birthday, members of the listening audience showed up at the WPOP studio with cakes they'd baked for this fictional character that Ken Griffin concocted. "Fats" and "Rocky" were characters on Ken Griffin's show for years, and the audience loved their "real" marital feuding. I used to sit in the newsroom and sketch out "bits" for the couple, which Ken would then realize on-air extemporaneously. That was part of his genius.*

On September 7, 1966, WPOP hired the outrageous Lee "Baby" Simms to host the night show, moving Ken to the afternoon drive shift. At that same time, Dick Robinson was ready to move into a daytime sales position. It was then that Charlie Parker pulled off a brilliant strategic move by replacing Robinson with his primary competitor—Ken Griffin—whom he enticed to move over to rival WDRC.

WPOP listeners came close to mutiny when Griffin and his cohorts "Fats Phontoon" and "Rocky Hill" jumped ship for POP's fierce rival WDRC. Ken's last official WPOP assignment was co-hosting a Hollies concert at the State Amory with WDRC's Long John Wade on Friday October 7, 1966.

For an in-depth interview with Ken Griffin, please see the appendix.

Long John Wade

John Wade was born on New Year's Eve 1939. He attended New Hampshire's New Hampton School, where he became interested in radio. John ran the school radio station, served as president of the radio club and was active in dramatics. He attended Boston University and worked at several Boston-area stations, including WSPR in Springfield, Massachusetts.

While working in Springfield as "Johnny Midnight," John got a letter inviting him to an audition for a job at Hartford's WDRC.

Charlie Parker had him change his on-air name to "Long John" in reference to his six-foot, four-inch height.

Long John's arrival at Big D officially marked the transition from the "Friendly Five" to the "Swinging Six." A feature on his show was a countdown of the Top 13 records on the *Swinging Sixty Survey* every Monday afternoon. He hosted the *LJW Fling* during his entire stay, mostly from 4:00 to 8:00 p.m. (but briefly from 3:00 to 6:00 p.m.).

John became a regular instructor at Dick Robinson's Connecticut School of Broadcasting and later started his own broadcasting school in Philadelphia.

Don Wade

Born on February 20, 1941, Don Wade's real name was Don Maxfield Wehde. Don attended New Hampshire's New Hampton School (class of 1959), where he was co-president of the radio club. He began college at William and Mary but then transferred to Boston University. It was at BU that Don really became interested in pursuing a career in radio.

WDRC's disc jockey brothers. *Left*: Long John Wade; *right*: Don Wade. *Courtesy of Ed Brouder.*

Don was the younger brother of Long John Wade and was sometimes called "Long Don Wade," especially because of his six-foot, five-inch height. At WDRC, he initially replaced Shannon as the staff utility man, hosting Saturdays from 1:00 to 4:00 p.m. and Sundays from 7:00 p.m. to midnight.

Also known as "Don Juan," Wade worked the WDRC morning show beginning in March 1966. His voice characterizations were used to introduce a number of colorful and humorous guests. Don soon became one of WDRC's most popular on-air personalities.

Like his brother (Long John Wade), Don spent time with the Beatles, shooting home movies of the Fab Four as they filmed *Help*. Contest winners were treated to a special showing of *Help* in August 1965.

Sandy Beach

Donald N. Pesola was a native of Lunenberg, Massachusetts, and was a graduate of Lunenburg High School (class of 1958). He went on to study radio at Boston's Leland Powers School (class of 1961). Donald was working at WSPR (Springfield) when Charlie Parker hired him for WDRC's 10:00 a.m. to 1:00 p.m. shift, renaming him Sandy Beach. Sandy later did 1:00 to 4:00 p.m., then noon to 3:00 p.m., before taking over the morning drive show after the departure of Don Wade in October 1967.

Sandy Beach. *Courtesy of Ed Brouder.*

Sandy's unusual laugh was recorded as a sound effect and was aired for many years on WDRC.

After DRC, Donald was an on-air personality at WKBW (Buffalo) and several other radio stations. Sandy Beach retired from WBEN (New York) on July 20, 2020, after a sixty-year radio career.

Ron Landry

Born in Louisiana but raised in Washington D.C., "Buffalo Ron" was an original member of WDRC's "Friendly Five."

Left: Ron Landry, 1964; *right*: Ron Landry at WDRC in 1965; note his handmade door-slamming machine. *Courtesy of Ed Brouder.*

He hosted the *Live and Lively* morning drive show during his six years at WDRC. From 1965 to 1966, Ron also hosted *Scene 18* every Friday night at 6:00 p.m. on the Connecticut TV station WHCT.

Ron was a master of character voices, including "Hemingway Monroe," "Dan Press," "Charlie," "Doug Weedwell" and beatnik "Geets Romo." He recorded their voices during records and then played them back and had a "live" conversation with the characters.

Ron moved to the West Coast, and during the early 1970s, he issued a number of successful comedy albums with broadcast partner Bob Hudson. Hudson and Landry's "Ajax Liquor Store" was played on WDRC.

Ron's career moved into television, where he was a very successful member of the writing teams of the TV shows *Benson, Flo, The Red Foxx Show, Szysznyk* and *Gimme a Break!*.

Ron Landry released his last comedy album with comedian Tom Beiner in 1989.

Bill "FM" Stephens

Charlie Parker rescued and saved my radio future.
—*Bill Stephens, former WDRC air personality*

The following are Bill "FM" Stephens' recollections—in his own words—of working at WDRC:

My road to Hartford began in 1973, weeks after ending my correspondence course with the Columbia School of Broadcasting. At the time, I was working as a board operator and staff announcer at Boston's WRYT.

I was reading the old Radio 'n' Records *trade newspaper every week, and one day I noticed an ad by WCCC AM/FM in Hartford that was looking for a weekend disc jockey. I had never had a DJ show, but I frequently used the production studio at WRYT to record practice DJ shows. I felt ready to jumpstart my career, so I threw together an audition tape and sent the tape to WCCC.*

A few days later, WCCC program director Rusty Potz called and invited me to come down for an interview. When I spoke with him, he said he needed an overnight jock on Sunday nights, which paid $100. Rusty was surprised that I would be willing to make the drive from Boston every Sunday night for only $100.

I told him I really wanted to be a Top 40 DJ. Despite the low pay, I felt it was a great opportunity for me given the fact that I had so little experience. And so, in the winter of 1973, Bill Stephens became "Boston Bill" on WCCC every Sunday night at midnight.

During the summer of 1976, I was the program director and afternoon host on WCOD in Hyannis.

WDRC's Charlie Parker would listen around to the different radio stations on the dial wherever he traveled, scouting for new talent. In August 1976, Charlie tuned to WCOD and heard the midday host, Len Thomas, and later, me. A few days later, he contacted both Len and myself, asking if we'd like to come to Hartford and audition for a gig on WDRC.

Len was blown away since he was from Connecticut and very familiar with Big D. I knew what a fantastic program director Charlie was and working for him would be a terrific opportunity. And I knew WDRC was a big dog in Hartford.

Len was hired for WDRC-AM for middays. When I auditioned, I tried to let some of that Boston Bill schtick blend in, and Charlie was digging it. He knew about some of my bits so he knew I could be off-the-hook.

After consulting with Dave Overson (who was operating the board for my audition), Charlie decided I would be a great morning disc jockey, replacing Jack Morgan.

My first stint at WDRC ended two weeks before Christmas in 1976. I happened to mention on the air that for some reason I sounded "slurpy" on the radio and apologized that my voice was a little too "moist." I took a phone call from this young kid who advised me to smoke some weed, saying it will give me "dry mouth" and that should fix it. I thought it was pretty humorous, and it went on the air.

WDRC's GM at the time, Dick Korsen, heard my conversation with the pot-smoking kid and did not approve. Remember, this was 1976 and getting high was akin to heroin addiction. When my shift ended, so too did my stay at WDRC. Korsen fired me on the spot.

That same year, I moved to Los Angeles at the behest of another WDRC legend, Ken Griffin, who had opened a broadcasting school and DJ placement service out there. In the span of just over a year, I was on the air at several California radio stations. But I did not like California for a number of reasons and longed to be back on the East Coast.

To my surprise, Charlie Parker called me in April 1978, and asked me how I was doing in LA. I told Charlie that I was actually considering giving up the business to become a car salesman. Hearing this and wanting to help, Charlie got me in touch with Joey Reynolds, who at the time was an artist and repertoire agent for a major record label. Joey took me to lunch at the very swanky Palms Restaurant and gave me some terrific advice. He was great.

Soon after, Charlie asked if I'd like to come back to WDRC and do the 7:00 p.m. to midnight shift. I couldn't get back to Hartford fast enough!

It was then that Charlie Parker gave me the name Bill "FM" Stephens (aka "funky monkey"), and I brought along my imaginary associate "Lance Krindleman" as a regular visitor.

Charlie Parker had rescued and saved my radio future, plain and simple.

Left: WDRC's Bob Marx, Bill "FM" Stephens, unidentified, Tom Kelly and Brad Davis, 1977; *right*: Bill "FM" Stephens. *Both courtesy of Bill Stephens.*

I truly enjoyed my years on the radio in Hartford at both WCCC and WDRC. They were wild and wooly times in Top 40/personality radio, and I do miss those days.

Grahame Winters

Grahame Winters joined WDRC as promotions director in 1992. She's no stranger to the radio business. Her parents met while working at WPOP in the mid-1960s. Her father, the late Bill Winters, was a WPOP on-air personality for several years working the afternoon drive. Her mom, Marcia Win, played the role of "Miss Fox," the on-air secretary to morning drive host Woody Roberts.

Grahame's first on-air shift was during WDRC-FM's fortieth anniversary weekend in August 2000. The family's radio tradition continued when Grahame married WCCC overnight personality Jeff Slater.

Grahame became DRC's assistant program director in 2003 and was promoted to program director in August 2008. In late 2009, Grahame began hosting the 7:00 p.m. to midnight music show. She then inherited the midday shift after the departure of Larry Wells in October 2011. She worked at WDRC until July 7, 2014. Since then, Grahame Winters has been doing voice tracks for Koffee-FM in Cape Cod, Massachusetts.

Other Popular WDRC On-Air Radio Personalities

BRADLEY FIELD (real name Kenneth William Sasso) was born in Queens, New York. Sandy Beach referred to Field as "Andy Panda." He was also known as "Bradley Bucket." Field worked the afternoon drive. Bradley Field worked at WDRC from August 1967 to June 18, 1969.

JOE HAGER (born January 17, 1945) graduated from Camden (NJ) High School (class of 1963). He attended Rutgers University, where he got involved with campus radio station WRSU. Prior to WDRC, Hager was an on-air personality for several radio stations, including Waterbury's

Bradley Field. *Courtesy of Ed Brouder.*

Disc jockeys Joe Hager and Al Gates in the WDRC buggy. *Courtesy of Ed Brouder.*

WWCO and New Haven's WAVZ. At WDRC, he began working the 10:00 a.m. to 3:00 p.m. shift. His high-energy style made him a perfect replacement for Ken Griffin on the night shift beginning on April 13, 1970. On radio, Joe went by the names "Highgear Hager" and "Joe Beamer."

AL GATES hailed from Hamburg, New York, and attended Ithaca College. He later traveled the world as a NATO photojournalist and also worked for a time as a commercial artist. At WDRC, Al replaced Jim Jeffrey. Al Gates's routines included his duck "Feathers," "Akbar Mytie," "Mary Margaret" and "Readings with Charles."

BOB DECARLO attended Pennsylvania State University, where he began his radio career at the college radio station. DeCarlo worked at WDRC for a little over a year as DRC's morning man.

GARY DEGRAIDE had his own show on Fridays from 3:00 to 6:00 p.m. and Saturdays from 10:00 a.m. to 3:00 p.m. DeGraide worked at WDRC for almost two years.

LEE VOGEL replaced Joel Cash as host of the 9:00 a.m. to noon show on WDRC. The show was known as *The Voice of Vogel*. Lee arrived at Big D the same week as Joey Reynolds, who he already knew since they worked together in Buffalo. One of Lee's routines was a "Date with the D.J." The winner of the contest was treated to a Louis Armstrong concert at Hartford's Bushnell Memorial. Vogel also worked the 7:00 a.m. to noon shift on WDRC.

AARON SHEPARD (born August 19, 1932) graduated from Boston University. "Arnie" worked alongside Joe Barbarette in the Earwitness Newsroom. He found a way to work radio fun into the news by hosting and producing *Feature*, a series of silly questions designed to evoke unusual listener reaction.

JIM HARRINGTON (born James Kane Harrington on April 20, 1948) was one of the more popular personalities on WDRC. Jim began as the midnight to 6:00 a.m. host on WDRC-FM. He held every shift at one time or another. Harrington eventually pursued a screenwriting career, which landed him a stunt role in the hit movie *Jaws*. WDRC's Jay McCormick also

Aaron Shepard. *Courtesy of Ed Brouder.*

worked on the film as an extra. Jim appeared on the television soap opera *As the World Turns* and numerous national TV commercials. Harrington also developed the country's first home shopping program on a cable company in New Haven, Connecticut.

WDRC's Jim Harrington (*left*) and Pete Sullivan. *Courtesy of Ed Brouder.*

Pete Sullivan was born in Sioux Falls, South Dakota, but grew up in New Jersey. He was a graduate of Paramus High School and the American Academy of Dramatic Arts in New York City. Pete replaced Tom Hopkins on WDRC's morning show, 6:00 to 10:00 a.m. Sullivan often joked with news anchor Walt Dibble and was known for his voice impressions, including the leprechaun who dropped in at 7:20 every morning to announce, "They're after me Lucky Charms!"

Charlie Tuna (real name Art Ferguson) is one of the best-known voices in radio. At age sixteen, Art joined the local radio station where he grew up, in Kearney, Nebraska. For several years (April 2010–July 2014), Charlie Tuna's syndicated music show aired Sunday nights on WDRC-FM from 6:00 p.m. to 11:00 p.m. Ferguson spent most of his career as a Los Angeles personality and was awarded a star on the Hollywood Walk of Fame in 1990. He was also an announcer on several television shows, including: *The Mike Douglas Show* and *Scrabble*.

6

WPOP

WPOP Background

Early on, WPOP (a.k.a. POP radio) went through several name changes, beginning in 1935 when it was first licensed to air as WMFE-1380 (in New Britain). The call letters were almost immediately changed to WNBC, and the station soon moved to Hartford. In 1944, the call letters were changed again to WHTD. Subsequent call letters were WONS (1946) and WGTH (1953). Finally, the station became known as WPOP-1410 in 1956, when it focused on news, music and special events. WPOP became a true Top 40 station beginning in 1958. TV celebrity Merv Griffin purchased the station in 1972. However, on June 30, 1975, WPOP abandoned music programming and became a news and information station and has been referred to as News Radio 1410 WPOP.

Note: For some young radio listeners at the time, the fierce rivalry between WPOP and WDRC during the 1960s and early 1970s proved to be exciting and entertaining, especially hearing the reaction of some of the on-air radio personalities who worked at the two stations. There was a great deal of pride on the line to be the state's number one radio station, at least as it related to the targeted teenage audience.

WPOP on-air personalities at Halloween party, 1967. *Left to right*: Dan Clayton, Woody Roberts, Miss Fox, Bill Bland, Gary Girard (overnights) and Bill Winters. Lee Simms is absent from this photo because he was on-air when the picture was taken. *Courtesy of Marcia Win.*

Notable WPOP On-Air Radio Personalities

Danny Clayton

I relish the days of the competition between WPOP and WDRC. The day-to-day, back-and-forth counter program we did between DRC and POP was all-consuming. Every morning, that's what motivated me, always wondering, "How do we beat those guys?"

—Danny Clayton/Ken Wolt

Ken Wolt used several names during his radio career, including "Danny Clayton," "Darlin' Dan Clayton" and "Dangerous Dan." He joined WPOP in 1967, working the 3:00 p.m. to 7:00 p.m. shift (later 3:00 p.m. to 6:00 p.m.).

Ken frequently recorded his programs and mailed them to American troops in Vietnam to give them a taste of home. Listeners would send in the name of their loved ones in the service and tape a special message in the program.

In 1968, Danny Clayton replaced Woody Roberts as WPOP's program director.

Ken Griffin

I created "Fats" and "Rocky" to have somebody to talk to on the air. They had two kids, "Pebbles" and "Pebblina."

—*Ken Griffin*

Danny Clayton recording his WPOP show for Connecticut soldiers in Vietnam. *Courtesy of Ken Wolt (Danny Clayton).*

Joseph T. Mulhall Jr. was born on June 29, 1937, in Waterbury, Connecticut.

Using his persona "Ken Griffin," he cut his radio teeth at all three AM stations in his hometown of Waterbury (WBRY, WATR and WWCO). He then moved on to several other radio stations, including stations in Boston and Springfield, Massachusetts. Ken came to WPOP from WHYN in Springfield. Within weeks of starting at POP radio, Ken was also hosting a weekly TV show on Channel 18 in Hartford.

Ken was accompanied each night by "Fats" ("Phats") Phontoon, "the lovable weather balloon"; her boyfriend/husband, "Rocky Hill"; and also their two kids, named "Pebbles" and "Pebblina." The lengthy dialogues of Fats and Rocky Hill were all voiced, live, by Ken.

At one point in 1965, Griffin challenged listeners to count the records between 8:00 and 9:00 p.m.—if he played fewer than twenty per hour the first caller would collect $100.

Ken was famous for his Order of the Black Socks, for which membership cards were distributed. If you were spotted wearing black socks, you won a handful of 45s from WPOP's Good Guys. Prior to moving to WDRC, Ken's last official WPOP assignment was co-hosting a Hollies concert at the State Amory with WDRC's Long John Wade on Friday October 7, 1966.

Ken spent time in Hollywood as the press agent for movie star Sal Mineo.

Ken Griffin was one of Connecticut's most popular radio personalities and was a favorite with teenage listeners.

For an in-depth interview with Ken Griffin, please see the appendix.

Joey Reynolds

When I was a kid, I swear I was Joey's biggest fan. My girlfriend and I used to take a bus from East Hartford to Buffalo to see Joey when he moved to WKBW, as we didn't have our driver's license yet.
—Marcia Win (formerly "Miss Fox" on WPOP)

Legendary disc jockey Joey Reynolds was born in Buffalo, New York. He joined the WPOP on-air staff in 1962 after working in six other radio stations. At POP, Joey took control of the 7:00 p.m. to midnight shift, anointing himself as the Emperor of the Night People.

Even at that time, his wild reputation was legendary. After being let go by WKBW in his hometown of Buffalo, Joey decided to send a message to management. Prior to walking out of the studio on his last day, he nailed shoes to the program director's door with a note that read, "Now, fill these."

Reynolds's show was known for its humor, engaging banter and his ability to connect with his listening audience. He is probably best known for his wacky routines and his hysterical ad-libbing, much to the delight of his legions of fans.

Joey Reynold's vibrant on-air personality and entertaining style during his time at the station has left a lasting impression on Connecticut radio. His stay at WPOP was fairly brief, but Joey is fondly remembered by his fans even to this day.

In the 1960s, Joey's theme song was sung by Frankie Valli and the Four Seasons in the style of their hit "Big Girls Don't Cry."

Woody Roberts

Woody and I did the first two-person morning show in Hartford radio. At that time there were no women on Top 40 stations. My maiden name was Fox. Of course, Woody jumped on that, so our skits involved Woody and his secretary, "Miss Fox"
—Marcia Win, "Miss Fox"

⊙ ⊙ ⊙

Woody was a programmers' programmer. Philosophical but spot on.
—TJ Lambert, former WPOP disc jockey

Before he left WPOP, Woody Roberts gave me a "master class" in programming that I adhered to for the rest of my career.
— Bob Paiva, prior to becoming WPOP program director

Robert H. Bracken (better known as "Woody Roberts") hailed from Johnstown, Pennsylvania. When Woody joined WPOP, he worked as the morning drive host and program director. He previously worked at San Antonio's KONO and KTSA radio stations. It was there that Woody worked with Lee "Baby" Simms. He and Lee Baby became very close friends, even buying a cabin cruiser together.

Woody's cast of characters included his lovely and competent on-air secretary "Miss Marcia Fox" (real name Marcia Win) and Dick

Woody Roberts. *Courtesy of Ed Brouder.*

Orkin's "Chickenman." Also, Woody regularly checked the "Weather Knee Forecast."

He was a member of WPOP's Good Guys basketball team, which played benefits at schools around Hartford, Connecticut.

Lee "Baby" Simms

Lee "Baby" Simms was a unique, beloved on-air personality with a legion of fans.

—Bob Paiva

Gilmore LaMar Simms was born on August 24, 1943. He began his radio career at age eighteen. Simms was a renowned disc jockey better known as Lee "Baby" Simms. At one point, Lee worked with WPOP's Woody Roberts at San Antonio's KONO. He and Woody resigned from KONO and moved to cross-town rival KTSA in April 1966.

On September 7, 1966, Lee and Woody joined the WPOP on-air staff, with Woody hosting the morning drive and Lee replacing Ken Griffin on the 7:00 p.m. to midnight shift. Griffin moved to POP's afternoon drive shift but jumped ship to rival WDRC a month later.

After reading a pimple cream commercial during his first show, Lee unleashed a tirade of angry calls when he graphically described how terrible it is to get close to a girl "only to have a pimple pop."

While at WPOP, Simms would frequently interrupt songs that were playing and go on extended tirades to complain about long hair, sloppily dressed teenagers, rude people and other annoyances. He was quoted in local newspapers saying, "I don't like anything, including Hartford." Lee was the first to call downtown Hartford's new Constitution Plaza the "Constipation Plaza." He got into trouble for telling his listeners to go to Constipation Plaza and have a snowball fight there. Lee's ad-libs were legendary. On the air, he would make controversial statements, such as, "I'm rude and crude and impolite because you are."

Simms worked at POP from September 1966 to part of 1967. He left WPOP in 1967 and went back to KTSA in San Antonio and then KONO. Lee briefly returned to WPOP in December 1967 through January 1968 to host the 6:00 p.m. to 9:00 p.m. shift. Note: Lee's last on-air appearance in Hartford was on September 21, 1974, during the kickoff of a local Hartford radio station that featured an oldies format.

Lee Baby was on the air for forty years and retired in 2001. He had a total of forty-two jobs as a disc jockey at thirty-three stations and nineteen radio markets—and was fired twenty-five times.

As was the case with Joey Reynolds, Lee Baby's act was quite different than what Connecticut listeners were used to hearing.

Simms was known for his energetic and entertaining style, incorporating many comedy routines into his radio show, which made for good listening. Lee Baby was certainly one of the most colorful—and controversial—disc jockeys in radio history.

Lee "Baby" Simms was a legendary, beloved on-air personality to his legions of fans, despite his controversial statements and antics—or maybe because of them.

Dick Heatherton

After stops at WBIC and WGLI (both in Long Island), twenty-three-year-old Dick Heatherton joined the WPOP on-air staff replacing Lee "Baby" Simms. His WPOP initiation consisted of co-hosting Woody Roberts's morning show. Following this, Dick initiated a forty-hour on-air marathon skit during which the other WPOP Good Guys were supposedly kidnapped.

His initial shift was 7:00 p.m. to midnight though he quickly moved to 9:00 p.m. to 1:00 a.m., where he was "King of the Kielbasa Country." While at WPOP, Dick promoted an album he recorded.

In March 1968, Dick appeared on a Dean Martin summer TV show with his sister, singer/actress star Joey Heatherton. When he returned, Dick worked the 6:00 p.m. to 9:00 p.m. shift at WPOP.

In July 1969, Dick made his third appearance on the Mike Douglas TV show, appearing with his sister Joey and his dad, a former big-band leader.

Heatherton left WPOP for Philadelphia's WFIL but returned for a month in the fall of 1970, where he debuted as "Monticello the Magnificent." He then left WPOP again for on-air jobs at a number of other radio stations.

Doug Ward

Doug Wardwell became interested in radio while he attended Boston University in the 1950s. Known as "Doug Ward" or "Doug the Bug," he was a disc jockey in WPOP's pop music infancy in the late 1950s. Doug worked the 2:00 p.m. to 5:30 p.m. shift. He presided over "Bug Clubs" and did many remotes at Crystal Lake Ballroom in Rockville, Connecticut, hosting the day's top recording artists (Rockville was Hall of Famer Gene Pitney's hometown).

Ron and His Rattletones recorded Doug Ward's instrumental theme song "Doug's Drag." *Author's collection.*

An outgrowth of the "Bug" was his overnight alter-image, the "Cool Ghoul," using different voices and guests artists via tape.

Doug Ward's theme song was "Doug's Drag," written and recorded by Rockville's Ron Cormier of Ron and his Rattletones.

NOTE: RON AND HIS Rattletones was the first band that Rockville legend Gene Pitney performed with on stage.

Rusty Potz

Rusty Potz seems to go together. Much more memorable than Bob Potz.
—Disc jockey Rusty Potz

Rusty Potz (Robert Lawrence Potz) earned an associate of arts degree from the University of Hartford in 1963. His pre-WPOP on-air experience was at Windsor's WSOR using the name Bob Potz. For a while, at WPOP he used the name "Ron Jackson." He also used the on-air names "Big Bob Russell" and "Bob Ryan." In 1966. He switched to his most memorable persona—"Rusty Potz."

In 1967, Rusty manned the 7:00 p.m. to midnight shift after the departure of Lee "Baby" Simms and before the arrival of Dick Heatherton.

After leaving WPOP, he was an on-air personality at New Haven's WAVZ and later worked at Hartford's WCCC during its "All Request" format, using the name Randy Potz.

Bob Paiva

Bob Paiva started working at WPOP in 1963 as assistant promotion director. Much of his work involved organizing shows at the Bushnell Auditorium and other venues. Some of the acts he brought to Hartford were Buffalo Springfield, the Moody Blues, Jimmy Hendricks, Paul Revere and the Raiders, the Beach Boys and several Dick Clark touring caravans featuring multiple acts. In 1964, he helped coordinate the Rolling Stones show at Dillon Stadium.

Bob had adopted the on-air name Bob "Marshall" when he was on the college radio station at the University of Rhode Island. The name was an homage to his then favorite disk jockey from New York, Jerry Marshall.

His on-air career at WPOP started in February 1966, using the name Bob Marshall. Later, WPOP president Joe Amaturo appointed Bob as community relations and public service director.

Bob was host of WPOP's late-night talk show, *Hotline*, later alternating the duties with Ed Clancy.

Using his real name, Bob was WPOP's music director and did occasional air shifts. In September 1972, he was promoted to program director.

Other Popular WPOP On-Air Radio Personalities

HOUND DOG. During WPOP's early days as a pop music station, George "Hound Dog" Lorenz was a fixture on Buffalo's WKBW radio station. From June 1957 to September 1958, he syndicated his show and WPOP aired it from 8:30 p.m. to 10:30 p.m.

Hound Dog would greet his listeners with this: "Welcome, Madtown cats and you out there in West and East Madtown as well. It's a pleasure to communicate with you cuddle bunnies and tomcats. I'd like to hear more about what's shakin' in the box shop, so communicate!"

> *The old people said rock 'n' roll wouldn't last six months. That's because they didn't understand it.*
> —*George "Hound Dog" Lorenz on rock 'n' roll*

MAD DADDY (real name Pete Myers), like Hound Dog before him, provided a nightly syndicated show on tape to WPOP. Originating from the mythical "Sponge Rubber Heaven," WPOP aired the show for a few months from 10:00 p.m. to midnight (October 31, 1963–January 1964). Myers began his radio career in the armed forces during World War II. He studied at the Royal Academy of Dramatic Art in London and worked for a time as an actor. While working at Cleveland's WHK radio, Myers perfected a frantic-paced rhyming act as "Mad Daddy."

THE GREASEMAN (Doug Tracht) was born in the Bronx and attended Ithaca College. After he got involved at the college radio station, WICB-FM, a colleague commented that he "was cooking with grease" and thus the "Greaseman" was born. After perfecting his act at several radio stations in the New York and Washington areas, he was hired by program director Dick Springfield to host WPOP's morning show. He portrayed a hick farmer "from cow country" and started and ended his show with the sounds of a tractor. The Greaseman, however, was a victim of the station's switch from music to the station's all-news format.

Scott Morgan (Lance Bruce Drake) assumed the name "Scott Morgan" when he was an on-air personality. Prior to his time at WPOP, Scott worked various shifts on rival station WDRC. He also worked at other Connecticut radio stations such as WBRY and WTBY (both in Waterbury, Connecticut).

Note: Lance Drake was a member of the popular Connecticut band known as the Blue Beats.

Lee Gordon (born Dana Lee Gordon) hailed from Manchester, New Hampshire (got his start in radio at WUNH-FM while a student at the University of New Hampshire in Durham). Lee worked at WPOP from February 4, 1974, to June 1975. He initially hosted the 10:00 a.m. to 3:00 p.m. shift. When Bob Craig joined the POP staff, Lee moved to the afternoon drive.

Gary Girard was born in Webster, Massachusetts, on October 3, 1943, and raised in East Hartford, Connecticut. He began his broadcast career at the University of Connecticut (Storrs), where he was involved with the college station, WHUS. Gary graduated from Boston University with a bachelor of science degree in broadcasting. Gary Girard joined WPOP in April 1964 and became a member of the "WPOP Good Guys." He hosted Saturday mornings from 6:00 a.m. to 11:00 a.m. and Sunday afternoons 3:00 p.m. to midnight. When Jerry Gordon left a few months later, Gary slid into the overnight shift and remained there for the rest of his stay. All told, Gary Girard was involved with WPOP for nearly five years. Gary and his wife, Lois, realized a longtime dream by obtaining a license for a new station. On November 30, 1995, they put WKCD-FM on the air, serving the Mystic/North Stonington area.

Frank Holler hailed from Hartford, Connecticut. He graduated from Weaver High School. He was also in the first class of the Connecticut School of Broadcasting. Frank was initially hired at WPOP in December 1967 as assistant to music director Bob Paiva. Part of his job involved distributing *GO* magazine (edited by Robin Leach). Frank began hosting Saturday and Sunday shifts on July 18, 1968. He left POP to join the navy in June 1969. While in the service, Frank worked at AFVN in Danang, Vietnam. His military obligation ended early, so Frank returned to WPOP on August 8, 1970, hosting weekends. Soon after, he moved into the full-time 7:00 p.m. to midnight slot replacing Doctor Jim Holiday. Later on, Frank turned the last hour of his program into an album hour, playing longer versions of many pop singles, reflecting the popularity of "heavier" sounds. When Frank got married in 1971, his ushers included fellow POP disc jockeys Ed Clancy, Gary Girard and John Scott. After WPOP, Frank Holler worked at WDRC-FM, where he instituted a Saturday night oldies show called *Jukebox Saturday Night*.

SHANNON (Robert George Tarring) was born on Long Island on August 20, 1938. He attended both Malverne High School and Wesfield (NJ) High School. Robert graduated from Rutgers University in New Jersey (class of 1961). In March 1980, he was named chief announcer on the Rutgers radio station. When he arrived at WPOP, Robert used the on-air name "Shannon." He replaced Chip Thompson as utility man among the WPOP "Swinging Six." In addition to hosting 1:00 p.m. to 4:00 p.m. Saturdays and 7:00 p.m. to 1:00 a.m. Sundays, Robert worked in the news department and filled in for other on-air personalities.

STEVE O'BRIEN (aka "Smilin' Steve-O") hosted WPOP's 6:00 p.m. to 9:00 p.m. shift at the time when the "WPOP Good Guys" became the "POP Boss Jocks." He was known for his fashion sense, sporting a collection of trendy bell bottoms, English-cut jackets, French cuff pullovers and Nehru-style jackets.

DEL RAYCEE was born Delbert G. Raycee on September 19, 1926. Del's on-air program (*Delzapoppin'*) took to the air from 6:30 to 9:00 a.m. In January 1959, Del was heard from 10:30 a.m. to noon and 1:15: to 2:00 p.m. After WPOP, Del was named station manager at WDEE in Hamden. In his later years, Del divided his time between Clinton, Connecticut, and Florida. Del died on December 7, 2018, at age ninety-two and was buried in the Connecticut Veteran's Cemetery in Middletown.

ALAN SCHAERTEL graduated from Hartford's Trinity College in 1956. Local newspaper articles sometimes referred to him as Allan Shortal. Alan worked at WPOP during the station's early days (1956–1957). He worked the afternoon shift from 1:45 to 5:00 p.m., playing Top 40 records. He was also the host for the station's *Wax Works Top 40 Review*.

Bob Scott began as a part-time disc jockey at WPOP. Scott soon became the host of the *Connecticut Ballroom* from 3:00 p.m. to 8:00 p.m., featuring pop record favorites. Incidentally, *Connecticut Ballroom* was established when WPOP was known as WONS in November 1951.

Sunny Shores (Sheldon Sunny Shores) was born in Pennsylvania and graduated from Cheltenham High School and Temple University. When he first began at WPOP "Sunny Shores" worked the Sunday night shift from 7:30 to 10:00p.m. In January 1972, Shores took over the overnight shift, replacing Ric O'Connor. His "flip-a-nickel" weather forecasts were a fan favorite.

Dick Stephens was born on July 27, 1929, in Worcester, Massachusetts. Prior to joining WPOP, Dick worked at Waterbury's WWCO (1958), New Haven's WNHC (1960) and WAVZ in New Haven (1963). Initially, he hosted the noon to 3:00 p.m. show, plus worked in promotions. At times, he did the news on WPOP, using the name "Dick Beech." On Sundays he hosted the noon to 4:00 p.m. (and later 10:00 a.m. to 1:00 p.m.) music shifts as Dick Stephens.

Lou Terri (born Louis Gualtieri) went by several names during his radio career, including "Lou Terri," "Loveable Lou" and "The Weird Beard."
    Lou Terri owns the distinction of playing music at WPOP longer than any other disc jockey (August 1959 to September 18, 1966). Early on, Lou attended the Northwest School of Broadcasting. He joined WPOP after a yearlong stint at Hartford's WDRC.

Mike Greene was hired by music director Danny Clayton to replace Tom Tyler on the 9:00 a.m. to noon shift (the hours were later changed to 10:00 a.m. to 1:00 p.m.). In September 1969, Mike moved to the 4:00 p.m. to 7:00 p.m. shift to replace Dick Heatherton.

Bob Craig began his full-time midday shift on December 30, 1974, after working as a WPOP fill-in. Bob's 2:00 to 6:00 p.m. show was the last WPOP local music show, as the station went all-news on June 29, 1975. Prior to WPOP, Bob worked at WDRC from March 16, 1970, to October 4, 1974. Bob Craig was known to his listeners for his smooth on-air style and engaging personality. As part of his routine, Craig would suggest some wild luncheon menus, such as eating cold spaghetti sandwiches smothered with slivered almonds on a hard roll.

WPOP's Mike Greene (*left*) and Bob Craig while working at WDRC. *Courtesy of Ed Brouder.*

SCOTT ST. JAMES was born Jim Hicks on January 25, 1943, in Lockport, New York. He actually began his radio career when he and a friend built an unlicensed radio station while attending South San Francisco High School in 1959. Using his radio name "Scott St James," Jim replaced Mike Greene at WPOP for the afternoon drive. Scott St. James opened each show with a train whistle, announcing, "The St. James Express is smoking!"

7

WDRC VERSUS WPOP

THE RIVALRY

In those days, it was "WAR" between POP and DRC.
—Dick Heatherton, former WPOP disc jockey

⊙ ⊙ ⊙

The competition for ratings in Hartford was intense. At the time, WDRC was the Top 40 leader followed by WPOP.
—Bill Stephens, former WDRC radio disc jockey

⊙ ⊙ ⊙

Growing up in Connecticut with my ear firmly glued to both a transistor and a bedroom nightstand radio, I was treated to the marvelous AM "radio wars" between WPOP (Kenny Griffin) and WDRC (Dickie Robinson) and, later, to the rise of great FM stations like WPLR and WHCN. It was pure magic!
—Christine Ohlman, the "Beehive Queen," recording artist/songwriter

Both Big D and POP had a long legacy of super personalities such as Lee "Baby" Simms, Joey Reynolds, Dick Robinson, Ken Griffin and so on. Not all disc jockeys had the ability to perform on-air antics on a regular basis. But for those on-air personalities who were expert at performing outrageous bits while being able to hold the listeners' attention (sometimes for long periods), those disc jockeys were usually encouraged, within limits, to do anything, say anything and keep "making it crazy," hoping to "out-personality" the competition.

8

WATR

Growing up in Waterbury, I was asked by local radio station WATR to perform one of the songs I had been practicing at home on my guitar. So, I went down to their studio and performed a cover version of the Lloyd Price song "Lady Luck." I was only ten at the time, and I thought it was cool that this station (WATR) encouraged local musicians, such as myself, who had no experience recording their music but just wanted to perform on the radio.

—Ray Lamitola, musician

WATR (1320 AM) was first licensed to air in 1934 and serves Waterbury and Connecticut's Naugatuck Valley. It is mainly a news/talk radio station.

Beginning in January 1986, *Tom Chute & You* entertained WATR listeners during the weekly morning drive. The show was hosted by general manager and program director Thomas J. Shute, who was in broadcasting for fifty-two years. Chute retired in 2023. News director Christopher M. Fortier, veteran regional journalist, anchors news reports through the morning drive.

Barbara Hart Davitt hosts the *Coffee Break* show four days a week. She recently celebrated fifty-nine years at WATR. In 2018, Davitt was inducted into the Connecticut Broadcasters Association Hall of Fame.

Talk of the Town, hosted by Tom Hill III, airs weekdays from 10:00 a.m. to noon. The show focuses on local and state issues. Previous hosts include Steven Noxon, Larry Rifkin, Ed Flynn, James Senich and Jay Clark. Frank Marro was news director at WATR.

Other popular on-air personalities who once worked at WATR include Dick McDonough (afternoon drive) and Bob Craig (various shifts).

Larry Rifkin

WATR 1320 has been the epicenter of the Waterbury community for ninety years. It is the station that mature folks listen to, and it has earned and owned the news and information mantle in the city for generations... My dad initially came to Connecticut to take a job at WATR. He was the program director and host there in the 1950s....From the beginning, WATR was a major part of our lives, first as my dad's work home, and then as a formidable rival to Waterbury's WWCO. Like my dad, WATR served as my work home when I was hired as a news/talk anchor on the station.

—*excerpts from the book* No Dead Air *by Larry Rifkin*

Like his father, Larry Rifkin worked at WATR as an anchor and host of WATR's popular radio program *Talk of the Town*. Later, Larry held a variety of significant and important positions with Connecticut Public Television, including program executive. In 1992, Larry Rifkin was instrumental in bringing Barney the Purple Dinosaur to the pinnacle of success. *Barney* was an instant hit on public television and quickly became one of the most popular children's programs in the history of public television.

9

WWCO

WWCO Background

WWCO, serving Waterbury, Connecticut, first went on the air in 1946. The station currently follows a news/talk information format.

During the 1960s and 1970s, WWCO was owned by Merv Griffin and operated as a Top 40 radio station. It was known at the time as 1240 Super Music C-O. The station evolved from Top 40 to an adult contemporary format referred to as "All-Star Music WWCO." From 1984 to 1989, the station aired a popular nighttime urban contemporary show called *Nightflight* hosted by Ricky J. Washington.

Eventually, WWCO became a news/talk radio station.

Over the years, local WWCO on-air personalities included Ken Griffin, the Mad Hatter, Wildman Steve Gallon, Bob Gilmore, Ed Flynn, Bob Rouge, Joe Cipriano (a.k.a. "Tom Collins"), Danny Lyons, Dr. Chris Evans and Bob Crager.

WWCO logo. *Courtesy of Danny Lyons.*

Notable WWCO On-Air Personalities

The Mad Hatter

The Mad Hatter was a bigger-than-life radio personality. At times, he would broadcast live from rooftops of Waterbury buildings and still draw crowds. He was bighearted and really connected with people from all walks of life. The Mad Hatter was a beloved on-air personality at WWCO.
—Danny Lyons, disc jockey

The Mad Hatter (real name Ed Maglio Jr) was one of the most popular disc jockeys on WWCO in Waterbury, Connecticut. He was a beloved local disc jockey known for his high-energy, humor, diverse music selection, distinctive voice, and his madcap on-air persona. The Mad Hatter show was a fan favorite—a highly interactive show in which he encouraged his listeners to sing along to the tunes he was playing or participate in his zany on-air routines. Wearing his top hat and smoking his cigar, the "Mad Hatter" was a beloved radio disc jockey during the 1960s and 1970s.

Tom Collins

As a young teenager growing up in Waterbury, I grew up listening to Tom Collins on WWCO. Having the opportunity to work with him

Helpin' Easter Seals
A contribution to a fund-raising drive for the Easter Seal Rehabilitation Center from Cindy Gargoni (right) is happily received by Danny Lyons, left, and Ed Maglio, the Mad Hatter, top radio station personalities, who sit on cakes of ice as a promotion for the fund-raiser at shoppers center Friday night. — Marens photo

Disc jockeys on ice plug for rehabilitation center

was a dream come true for me, especially because he was from my hometown of Waterbury. Despite becoming a very successful voice-over talent, Joe has not lost his small-town charm, which endears him to many, many people.

—Danny Lyons, disc jockey

Tom Collins (real name Joe Cipriano) hailed from Waterbury, Connecticut, and was a well-liked on-air personality at WWCO. Joe went on to become a popular and successful voice-over talent.

Opposite, left: WWCO disc jockeys Danny Lyons (*left*) and Mad Hatter (*right*). *Courtesy of Danny Lyons.*

Opposite, right: The Mad Hatter. *Courtesy of Danny Lyons.*

Right: Bob Rouge WWCO disc jockey. *Courtesy of Al Warren.*

Below: Danny Lyons (*left*) and Stefan Rybak (*right*). *Courtesy of Stefan Rybak.*

10

WCCC

WCCC Background

WCCC-AM (1290 on the dial) dates to 1948. The station, owned by local jeweler Bill Savitt, was originally located in West Hartford, but eventually the studios moved to Hartford, Connecticut.

WCCC's call letters stood for "We Cover Connecticut's Capitol." Early programming consisted of news, popular music of the day and sports. WCCC-FM (106.9 on the dial) was licensed in 1959. While the station went through a number of format changes, it is generally best known for the period of time the station programmed rock music (especially on FM). WCCC's all-request format was a popular feature among station listeners.

Howard Stern began his talk radio career at radio station WCCC in the late 1970s. Other notable hosts who worked at WCCC include Ken Griffin, Bob Crane, Rusty Potz, Sebastian, Bill Stephens and Bob Marx. WCCC's *Homegrown Program*, hosted by Slater and Jonny Promo, gave local bands in the Northeast an opportunity to perform on local radio.

Eventually, WCCC-AM ceased programming, and WCCC-FM changed to a noncommercial contemporary Christian radio station.

Notable WCCC On-Air Personalities

Bob Marx

Bob Marx (born Bart Mazzarella) hailed from New Britain, Connecticut. Bart used several names as an on-air personality, including: "Bob Marx," "The Bartman" and the "Italian Teddy Bear."

Prior to Hartford's WCCC, Bart worked at a number of other Connecticut radio stations, such as WLAE (Meriden), WKSS (Hartford) and WINF (Manchester). After WINF, Bart moved to Hartford's WDRC, where he hosted the 10:00 a.m. to 3:00 p.m. show from 1975 to 1983.

Note: Bart Mazzarella was the bass player for a popular Connecticut band known as the Detroit Soul. The band formed in 1965 and consisted mainly of local high school students from New Britain and Pulaski high schools. Band members were Bart Mazzarella/Bob Marx (bass), Peter Villano (Hammond B-3 organ), Joey Verillo (saxophone), Ronnie Carrubba (drums), Richard (Skip) Blankenburg (trumpet), Angelo Marian (trumpet) and Sal Lanares (from South Windsor, lead vocals). "All of My Life" by the Detroit Soul was a big hit in the United Kingdom and a regional hit in the United States. The song was used in the movie *Soulboy* and was featured on its soundtrack.

Bill Nosal

Bill Nosal was born in Glastonbury, Connecticut, and was a 1963 graduate of Glastonbury High School. In the '70s, he was an on-air radio personality for a few Connecticut radio stations, including WCCC, where, for a time, he was the program director.

Note: Prior to his radio days, sixteen-year-old Nosal wrote and recorded "My Prayer," under the name "Billy James." The song was released by Billy James and the Stenotones in 1961. The record did very well on New England charts, staying on the charts for thirteen weeks and peaking at no. 2 in Connecticut. The song also reached the Top 40 in Worchester and Top 50 in West Springfield, Massachusetts. The Stenotones consisted of several female Connecticut singers.

In 1962, "Meant for Me" and its B side "It's the Twist" were recorded by Billy James and the Crystal Tones. The Crystal Tones were a doo-wop vocal harmony group from New Britain, Connecticut.

James was also a member of the Connecticut band the Reveliers. In 1964, the Reveliers released the rocking instrumentals "Part III" and "Maureen." The band was led by Jerry Crane (guitar) and Billy James (organ). The Reveliers' instrumentals were recorded at the Al Soyka Studios in Somers, Connecticut.

Billy James appeared on *Connecticut Bandstand* and the Brad Davis TV shows.

Other Popular WCCC Radio Personalities

STEPHEN KANE (real name Stephen Harold Capen) was born on February 28, 1946, in Brockton, Massachusetts. He attended Rockland High School (class of 1964) and began his radio career at the radio station of Boston's now defunct Cambridge School/Graham Junior College. At WCCC, Stephen hosted the morning drive from 1969 to 1970. Kane previously worked at WDRC.

STONEMAN (born Joseph J. DeMaio in New Haven, Connecticut) attended the University of Bridgeport. His on-air name was the "Stoneman." DeMaio

Bob Marx (*left*) and Stephen Kane while working at WDRC. *Courtesy of Ed Brouder.*

was a well-known disc jockey at Hartford WCCC-FM. Previously, he was an on-air personality at WPLR-FM from 1969 to 1981.

GEORGE FREEMAN hailed from Youngstown, Ohio. George worked in the news department at a number of radio stations. Prior to joining the WCCC staff, George was the news director at Hartford's WDRC (late 1959–1962).

BEEF STEW (real name Stew Crossen) was an on-air personality at WCCC for thirteen years, beginning in 1995. He played a mix of contemporary and classic blues-rock. "Beef Stew" hosted the six-hour on-air program *Sunday Night Blues* on WCCC.

11
WICC

My mom, dad and I always listened to the radio in our home. I was interested in music since age five and listened to radio station WICC. I also started drum lessons then as well. WICC had a segment called Talent Roundup. *I switched to guitar at age ten, and about two years later I was on* Talent Roundup *with my band called the Mods. WICC played a large variety of music. We would hear such diverse artists as the Beatles, Frank Sinatra, the Rolling Stones, Little Richard, Nat King Cole, Elvis, James Brown, Patty Page, the Kinks, Hank Williams Sr., just everybody!!! I believe that made me a well-rounded musician and helped shape my career to work with so many diverse performers as I did!*

—*Al Ferrante, musician*

WICC Background

WICC (600 on the dial) was licensed to Bridgeport, Connecticut, in 1926 (ninety-eight years ago as of this writing). It was Bridgeport's first radio station and one of the first stations in Connecticut. Its call letters stand for "Industrial Capital of Connecticut."

In the 1960s and 1970s, WICC was considered a middle-of-the-road station, featuring pop/rock music that was popular at the time. For over ten years, Tony Reno and Mike Bellamy were hosts of the *Tony & Mike in the Morning* on WICC-AM.

Al Warren while working at Waterbury's WWCO, 1963. *Courtesy of Al Warren.*

Other popular on-air personalities who worked at WICC include Storm N. Norman (who later was a radio personality on WEBE), Al Warren, Walt Dibble, Tim Quinn, Jim Buchanan, John LaBarca and Frank Holler (who also was a radio disc jockey on Hartford's WPOP and WDRC radio stations).

Eventually, WICC became a news and information station. Currently, Paul Pacelli hosts the popular *Connecticut Today* show on WICC.

Notable WICC On-Air Personalities

Bob Crane

Bob Crane was an on-air radio personality on WICC from 1951 through 1956. Crane was born in Waterbury, Connecticut, and graduated from

Stamford (CT) High School in 1946. He was a member of the Connecticut and Norwalk (CT) Symphony Orchestras. Bob Crane is best known for his role as Colonel Robert Hogan in the hit TV series *Hogan's Heroes*.

Walt Dibble

Walt Dibble hailed from Greenwich, Connecticut. He attended high school in Stamford and Bridgeport's New England School of Radio (in 1948).

Dibble arrived at WICC in Bridgeport after working at Stamford's radio station WSTC. He then moved on to New Haven's WAVZ. Walt subsequently moved to Hartford's WDRC, where he replaced Joe Barbarette as news director. After DRC, Dibble spent twenty years as news director at WTIC in Hartford. At WTIC, Walt worked with the legendary Bob Steele and also Ray Dunaway.

When his newscasts included Cincinnati Reds baseball scores, Walt had more than the usual interest, since his son—Rob Dibble—was a pitching star for the Reds.

Paul Pacelli

Paul Pacelli described his long radio broadcasting career in his own words:

> *I was always fascinated by radio as a child and knew from an early age that radio broadcasting was what I wanted to do.*
>
> *When I attended Boston University (class of 1984), I was a student radio station staffer there for four years. I've been working steadily in commercial radio since 1984.*
>
> *I have done it all and have worked with wonderful people, many of whom have become lifelong friends. Some of my on-air broadcasting assignments have included: news anchoring/reporting, traffic, sports and play-by-play. My current on-air job is as the talk show host of* Connecticut Today *on radio station WICC, as well as a national news anchor.*
>
> *To this day—even with all the current innovations and high-tech—I believe the spoken word is the most powerful form of communication.*
>
> *I've either worked at or been heard regularly on: WTBU (Boston University), WNHU (University of New Haven), WLIS, WSCR/*

Paul Pacelli, WICC. *Courtesy of Paul Pacelli.*

WQUN, WKCI, WAVZ, WCCC, the Connecticut Radio Network, WCNX, WNHC, WELI, United Stations Radio Network, WKSS, WHCN, WDRC-AM/FM, WMMW, WSNG, WWCO, WEBE, WTIC-AM, WSTC, WNLK, WPOP, WHYN, WPRO-AM, WHJJ, KXNT, Shadow Traffic and currently Fox News Radio, Fox News Headlines 24/7 and WICC-AM/FM.

Other Popular WICC Radio Personalities

JIM SCOTT was born on Long Island on February 28, 1943. He graduated from West Islip High School. Jim began his radio career at WMMM in Westport, Connecticut, and Waterbury's WWCO. He then moved to Hartford's WDRC, filling in for Jim Harrington on the 9:00 a.m. to 3:00 p.m. shift and later to the afternoon drive. After DRC, Jim joined WICC.

PETE ROSS hailed from Waterbury, Connecticut, and was a graduate of Thomaston High School, CW Post College and Connecticut School of Broadcasting. He worked at WDRC on three different occasions, using the

Jim Scott (*left*) and Pete Ross (*right*), WICC. *Courtesy of Ed Brouder.*

name "Pete Moss," and eventually switched back to Pete Ross. Pete joined Bridgeport's WICC staff after working at Hartford's WDRC and several other radio stations in the New York and Connecticut areas.

12

WELI

WELI Background

WELI was licensed to New Haven in October 1935 with studios in Hamden, Connecticut. WELI is a news and information radio station.

Notable WELI On-Air Personalities

Kent Clark

Kent Clark (born Walter Clement Pinto) has been a familiar voice on radio stations in Connecticut and other areas since 1967. Walt was born in Brooklyn, New York, but moved to Maine, where he graduated from the local high school in Old Town and gained experience on the radio station at school. He later attended the University of Maine.

Using the name "Kent Clark," Walt was a versatile on-air personality, working various shifts at the radio stations he worked in and spending most of his time in the news department. He worked at WDRC on three separate occasions. After DRC, Walt became an on-air personality at Hartford's WCCC. He then moved to Farmington's WRCQ. After WRCQ, Walt joined the New Haven's WELI radio staff.

In 1970, Walt became the director of the Stratford, Connecticut branch of Dick Robinson's Connecticut School of Broadcasting. He later became the director of the Hartford branch.

Jerry Kristafer

Jerry Kristafer (from Pennsville, New Jersey) was a popular host of the *WELI Morning Show* from 1998 to 2008, and he also served as program director. Jerry was an on-air personality at numerous other radio stations, including WDRC, WCCC, KC-101, WAVZ, WCDQ and WTLC.

13

WTIC

WTIC Background

WTIC (1080 on the dial) was licensed to Hartford, Connecticut, in 1924. It is a news and information radio station.

Notable WTIC On-Air Personalities

Bob Steele

Certainly the most notable radio personality on this station was Bob Steele, who spent sixty-six years at WTIC, most of them as the morning drive-time host. He joined WICC in 1936. *The Bob Steele Show* was a very popular program, especially in central Connecticut.

Bill Hennessey

Popular on-air personality Bill Hennessey hosted a midday show on WTIC in the 1950s and 1960s called *Hennessey—That's Me*. In 1975, Hennessey joined the staff at WDRC and was a co-anchor of the *WDRC Morning News* show (January 1975–June 1975) with Walt Dibble and Ted Dalaku.

Gary Craig

Gary Craig was an on-air personality on WTIC for over thirty years. He was the host of the popular *Craig and Company* show on WTIC.

Gary became a well-known radio personality for his "Phone Scams" segment. In these skits, he would make prank calls to unsuspecting individuals, adopting different personas and engaging in humorous conversations.

Steve Parker

Steve Parker is the on-air host of WTIC's Saturday morning show beginning at 5:30 a.m. Steve features news, sports, "Traffic & Weather Together on the 8s," plus interviews with a variety of news makers. Steve is the son of famed WDRC program director Charlie Parker.

NOTE: STEVE AND HIS sister Kathy (Parker) Morgan share their memories of their father, Charlie Parker, in the chapter titled "Disc Jockey Skits, Routines and Stories."

14

WAVZ

At WAVZ in 1970, I worked with and got to know well some great guys such as Bill Beamish, Ed Flynn, Tiny Markle, Bob Dark and Jay Crawford.

—Dick Kalt

Born in the Bronx, my first exposure to radio were the New York kings of the airwaves: WABC, WMCA and WINS.

When my family moved to New Haven, Connecticut, in 1968, my ears were glued to 1300 on the AM dial, WAVZ. All the DJs at WAVZ were distinct voices and personalities to me and were my broadcast heroes for many years. Many of these DJs moved on to the FM dial and bigger markets, while many became friends of mine—outside of radio. The radio was literally on in our house twenty-four hours a day (especially when there were call-in contests!).

Along with the songs they played, the stars of Connecticut radio helped compose the soundtrack of my life.

—Charles F. Rosenay, Professional Fun MC/DJ Music Entertainment

WAVZ Background

WAVZ-1300 AM served New Haven and the surrounding area. During the 1960s, the station played rock/pop music and competed with Hamden's

KOPS-MONAHAN COMMUNICATIONS

WAVZ logo. *Courtesy of Danny Lyons.*

WDEE (1220) and New Haven's WNHC for radio listeners. For the most part, WAVZ was the ratings winner.

WAVZ moved to a news and information station and eventually switched to a sports format.

As FM radio became more popular, the station's rock music format was shifted to sister FM station WKCI in 1979. WKCI had been an easy-listening station, but in the summer of 1979, it became KC-101 and played rock-oriented music. Some of the WAVZ personalities switched to KC-101.

Notable WAVZ On-Air Personalities

Tiny Markle

Erwin J. "Tiny" Markle was born in New Haven, Connecticut, on September 26, 1927. He graduated from Connecticut's Milford Academy and Bethany College in West Virginia. It was at Bethany College that Markle began his radio career when he became involved in the radio station at the college. Markle was a radio talk show host on a variety of radio stations for twenty-one years. His show was considered both entertaining and provocative. His local radio shows consisted of opinions and discussions about a wide variety of topics of interest to his listeners.

Markle worked at other Connecticut radio stations, including New Haven's WAVZ, along with WNAB and WICC (both in Bridgeport). While at WAVZ, Markle was the leader and bass player of a band that toured throughout New England. The band opened for headliners such as Nat King Cole, Count Basie and the Dorsey Brothers. His band performed frequently at Bridgeport's Pleasure Beach and Ritz ballrooms.

Left: WAVZ continued their music surveys into the late 1970s (July 2, 1979); *right*: WAVZ promotion showing disc jockey Danny Lyons interviewing Meatloaf. *Both courtesy of Danny Lyons.*

Ed Flynn

Ed Flynn was an on-air personality on WAVZ. In addition, Ed worked at a number of other Connecticut radio stations, including WELI, WWCO, WTIC, WMMW and WDRC. He was involved in broadcasting for fifty-five years.

Ed was also an instructor at Dick Robinson's Connecticut School of Broadcasting.

Bill Beamish

Bill Beamish had a successful career as a popular on-air personality at WAVZ in the 1960s and a member of the WAVZ "Straight Shooters." Bill was also a local TV personality, starring in a children's television program as "Space Commander 8" on WNHC-TV in New Haven, Connecticut.

TJ Martin

Through the 1960s and 1970s, Thomas James "TJ" Martin was an on-air personality at WAVZ, along with Bill Beamish and Ed Flynn.

Left: WAVZ. TJ Martin and Bill Beamish, 1971; *right*: Mike Holland. *Left, courtesy of Charles Rosenay; right, courtesy of Ed Brouder.*

Mike Holland

Michael Bouyea "Mike Holland" hailed from Forestville, Connecticut (a suburb of Bristol). Before joining the radio staff at WAVZ, Mike worked at radio station WWCO. After WAVZ, Mike moved to WDRC-FM doing the 7:00 p.m. to midnight shift. He then moved to WDRC-AM on April 8, 1973, replacing Gary DeGraide and working the same 7:00 p.m. to midnight shift.

Mike was a talented musician and frequently accompanied the records being played by beating on a drum pad. He always signed off his show by saying goodnight to his sweetheart, Karen, whose voice was heard on tape reciprocating.

Note: Michael was a member of a popular local garage band known as the Squires, formed in 1965. Three of the band members were 1965 graduates of Bristol Eastern High School. Another member graduated from Torrington High School in 1965. The Squires consisted of Michael Bouyea (vocals, drums, guitar), Thomas Flanigan (lead guitar, vocals), Kurt Robinson (organ), Jim Lynch (rhythm guitar) and John Folcik (bass). Later, Folcik and Robinson were replaced by Brian Blake (bass, vocals) and Paul Shea (organ, vocals).

"Going All the Way" by the Squires charted on Connecticut radio stations (No. 58 on WPOP) and was played on other area radio stations. The song appears on a compilation of garage rock recordings titled *Pebbles, Volume 1*. The Squires had a very loyal following in the local area.

Michael Bouyea later released several singles, including "The Fury," "Lover of the Night" and "I Can Wait." He eventually became an on-air personality on Toronto's CHUM radio station. Bouyea recorded a theme song for the Toronto Blue Jays baseball team titled "We Got the Blue Jays."

15

WEBE

WEBE Background

WEBE (107.9 FM) carries an adult contemporary music format and is known as WEBE 108. The station serves both the greater New Haven and Fairfield County areas.

Notable WEBE On-Air Personality

Danny Lyons

The time has literally flown by, and I still enjoy being part of the lives of so many great listeners in southern Connecticut.

—Danny Lyons

⊙ ⊙ ⊙

Danny Lyons really is WEBE. When the listeners think of the radio station, Danny is the first person that comes to mind. He truly is a master of his craft, and it is an honor to work with him every day.

—Keith Dakin, vice president of programming

Top, left: Danny Lyons broadcasting live, August 2, 2023; *right*: Storm N Norman, Dan Reeves (NY Giants coach) and Danny Lyons. Live broadcast at JFK Airport. *Left, author photo; right, courtesy of Danny Lyons.*

Middle, left: Storm N Norman Night with Paul McCartney; *right*: Danny Lyons WEBE. *Both courtesy of Danny Lyons*

Bottom, left: Danny's wife, Lynne; Ed Sheeran; and Danny Lyons. Mohegan Sun 2017; *right*: WEBE's Danny Lyons with Bon Jovi. *Both courtesy of Danny Lyons.*

Danny Lyons (real name Daniel Mangini) was born and raised in Waterbury, Connecticut. He attended Waterbury's Holy Cross High School.

Lyons began his radio career in 1972 (over fifty years ago). After working a few years at Waterbury's WWCO, Danny moved in 1978 to WAVZ-1300, where he hosted the afternoon shift. He subsequently moved to New Haven's WKCI (KC-101), Hartford's WTIC FM and New York's WNBC. Finally, he arrived and stayed at WEBE-108 on March 23, 1987, where he has been an on-air personality for over thirty-six years!

At WEBE, Danny hosts *The Lyons Den* weekdays from 10:00 a.m. to 3:00 p.m. For an in-depth interview with Danny Lyons, please see the appendix.

16
KC-101

In 1980, my solo recording "Only a Lonely Heart Sees" reached No. 14 in Connecticut thanks to requests from listeners of Connecticut radio stations such as KC101.
—Felix Cavaliere, Rascals, solo artist

KC-101 Background

WKCI-FM (better known as KC-101) was licensed to Hamden, Connecticut, a suburb of New Haven. KC-101 has a Top 40 contemporary music format.

KC101 logo. *Courtesy of Danny Lyons.*

Notable KC-101 On-Air Personality

Dr. Chris Evans

Dr. Chris Evans (real name Jack Camarda) was the morning show host on KC101. Joining Dr. Chris was his imaginary co-host "Hozay Smith," who was the corrupt mayor of Fogarea. The town of Fogarea was inspired by a sign on I-91 that warned drivers of a "fog area."

Felix Cavaliere visits KC101 in Connecticut. Pictured (l-r) are: Deby Gould, Epic Hartford Promotion Manager; Pete Salant, KC101 Operations Manager; Felix Cavaliere; Danny Lyons, KC101 midday man; Jerry Smallwood, National Director Epic Promotion.

Top, left to right: Deby Gould (Epic Hartford), Pete Salant (KC101 operations manager), Felix Cavaliere, Danny Lyons (KC101) and Jerry Smallwood (Epic). *Courtesy of Danny Lyons.*

Bottom, left: Danny Lyons; *right, left to right:* Danny Lyons, singer John Oates and Stefan Rybak, circa 1982. *Both courtesy of Stefan Rybak.*

Left to right: Chris Evans, Stacey Eisenberg and Danny Lyons. *Courtesy of Danny Lyons.*

17

WPLR

WPLR Background

WPLR (99.1) first aired in 1948 as WNHC-FM and was licensed to New Haven, Connecticut. The station can be received in much of the state, including Hartford and parts of Massachusetts. Also known as 99.1 PLR and "Connecticut's #1 Rock Station," WPLR has consistently achieved high ratings and has a loyal fan base in southern Connecticut.

Notable WPLR Disc Jockeys

Smith & Barber Show

Brian Smith and Bruce Barber were hosts of the *Smith & Barber* morning show. It was a popular program on WPLR-FM for almost eighteen years. In addition to playing classic rock music, the pair were known for their comic ad-libbing and wacky stunts.

At one point, Arbitron named the *Smith & Barber* show the no. 1 morning-drive program in the New Haven radio market.

The close of each show would feature the recorded bark of wonder dog Agnew.

Left: WPLR's Dick Kalt with Doobie Brothers, including Michael McDonald and Jeff "Skunk" Baxter; *right*: Jerry Lewis telethon held on the New Haven Green, hosted by WPLR. *Courtesy of WPLR's Dick Kalt, former general manager of New Haven's WPLR-FM.*

Brian Smith

Brian Smith and Pam Landry were the foundation of WPLR at one time. They built that radio station.

—Steve Zion, owner of WOW radio station

In his own words, Brian reminisced about his earlier on-air days and also his current radio venture with Pam Landry:

> *I grew up in Milford, Connecticut. The southwestern shoreline of Connecticut was a great place to grow up and enjoy radio and television. Living there, I was able to not only receive local Connecticut stations, but also the mother lode of broadcast news and entertainment—New York City. I listened to New York's WABC radio and their Top 40 format, and every afternoon I made sure I listened to WABC's Dan Ingram. Later on, I tuned into Imus in the Morning and Howard Stern on 66 WNBC.*
>
> *When I got my own car, I furnished it with the biggest and loudest stereo I could put together. It was then that I began listening to the rock and roll on-air personalities of the original WPLR in New Haven.*
>
> *In college, I worked some shifts as a news anchor on Yale's radio station, which led to my becoming general manager of the radio station at Southern Connecticut State University.*
>
> *I then had the opportunity to intern for Rick Allison, the morning radio personality at New Haven's WPLR. Eventually, I worked my way into a part-time air shift and then a full time slot in the overnights. In the mid-1980s, I inherited the morning show at WPLR. About a year later, Neal Mirsky, one of the original founders of MTV, became our new program director.*

It was then that Bruce Barber was brought in by Neal to be my morning show co-host. The Smith and Barber Morning Show *enjoyed an eighteen-year run. (We did spend a year in Tampa, Florida, at radio station 98 Rock until it changed ownership and its music format.)*

After a one year run at Tampa's radio station 98 Rock, The Smith and Barber Morning Show *returned to WPLR in 1990. Weird Al Yankovic sang our* Smith and Barber Morning Show *theme song.*

Our morning program became a ratings leader in Connecticut, and we were the number one radio program for many demographics in the state of Connecticut.

We had many notable moments during our morning show years at WPLR. Some of these included: being cast as extras on the Fox Network drama New York Undercover, *bringing a large group of listeners to the Bahamas' Atlantis Casino (twice), broadcasting a series of programs live from Florida's Universal Studios during winter breaks, airing weeklong beach broadcasts from the beautiful Connecticut shoreline (usually in West Haven) during the summers, performing our "Breakfast Band" on stage at Toad's Place and putting together an annual holiday show with bands and an odd assortment of entertainers at Wallingford's Oakdale Theater every December.*

Personally, I was rated the no. 1 most recognizable radio personality in Connecticut in the mid-1990s. It was an accolade that I humorously but

Brian Smith, in WOW radio studio, Wallingford, 2023. *Courtesy of Brian Smith.*

purposefully wasn't made aware of by station management until after I signed a new employment contract.

After WPLR, I had my own solo comedy and talk show on WICC-AM Bridgeport for seven years.

In 2011, I was a news anchor at New York City's 101.9 FM (FM News). When they called to ask me to work for them, I was sure they had the wrong guy since my career had been mostly comedy and music programming. I came to my senses during the phone call and took the job and enjoyed the work and our studios that looked out onto lower Manhattan and the Empire State Building. I was a news anchor simultaneously in New York City, Philadelphia and Chicago. I even appreciated the ninety-minute train commute into the city every day. I worked there for a year until the company was sold and we no longer were a news radio station.

In 2016, I began working at Quinnipiac University's commercial radio station, WQUN. They were a terrific and hardworking radio staff. We provided news, information and hit music for Hamden and surrounding towns. But then, in 2019, Quinnipiac University ended the operation of the radio station.

Steve Zion, the owner of Toyota of Wallingford, was part of our varied cast of on-air characters in our old WPLR days. He was sometimes known as the "ZMan." Steve provided us with custom-built monster trucks and fun prop automobiles, such as a van with a chamber of swirling prize money called the "Cash Blaster" and also the "Car-B-Q," an actual automobile that was half car and half barbecue grill. Steve is an avid race car fan who has been a track announcer for dragster competitions around the northeast and an emcee for NASCAR events throughout the country.

In 2022, Steve built a state-of-the art radio studio inside his Toyota of Wallingford dealership. He asked me to join him in a new radio venture, with the purpose of building a network of broadcast and online radio stations that would be another option for listeners who wanted something a bit different from the usual radio scene in Connecticut and New England.

So, we became WOW Radio, a combination of classic rock and Motown music, which also serves as a conduit for local friends and organizations to publicize their events.

Pam Landry, my friend and fellow broadcaster since my WPLR and WQUN days, has joined me at WOW. So now Pam and I co-host the Brian Smith and Pam Landry Show *and connect with our audience with the help of our producer and social media director, Holly Masi. Holly worked behind the scenes with us in our past radio stations. Our program is a mixture of topical and fun conversation, local celebrities, local information and music, with live in-studio musicians and top performers who are in the Connecticut area. The Brian Smith and Pam Landry on-air show broadcasts every weekday afternoon from 11:00 a.m. until 3:00 p.m.*

Pam Landry

I realize how fortunate I am to be able to reach people and connect with listeners through radio—and hopefully make someone's day a little better.
—Pam Landry

Pam Landry is a native of Westchester County, New York. She moved to Connecticut in 1990 and began working at Stamford's radio station WJAZ. After a couple years working part time at WPLR, Pam began full-time work at PLR as the midday disc jockey from 10:00 a.m. to 3:00 p.m. At this same time, she was WPLR's music director. Landry worked as a disc jockey at WPLR from 1993 until 2009.

Pam Landry in studio. *Courtesy of Pam Landry.*

Pam moved to radio station WXPK and then worked at radio station WQUN as the station's midday host/operations manager from 2016 to 2019. All along, Pam was busy with a number of other projects, including working in New York City as a producer of a syndicated rock radio show and fill-in host for VH1 Classic; working at Westchester radio station WXPK; writing scripts for Scott Shannon's syndicated *Hits Countdown Show*; doing voice-over work for Hartford's WNPR; and writing for the *New Haven Register* and *Patch* newspapers.

Pam Landry and Brian Smith have recently teamed up as co-hosts at WOW radio, broadcasting live online Monday through Friday 11:00 a.m. to 3:00 p.m.

Chaz and AJ

The *Chaz and AJ Morning Show* can be heard weekdays on WPLR 5:30 a.m. to 10:00 a.m. Their show features classic rock and a wide variety of discussion topics, including local interviews with all the big-name state politicians, AJ's

Chaz and AJ, WPLR. *Courtesy of Chaz.*

parody songs, Dumbass News, Flubble Friday, the daily Top 10 list and more. Chaz and AJ talk about what Connecticut is talking about.

As noted in the Chaz and AJ website:

> *Throughout the year, Chaz and AJ raise money for causes that matter to our community. Their annual "Toy Drive" raises, on average, over $150,000 in toys and monetary donations for five local children's charities. Their "Stand Up for Vets" event helps get automobiles for veterans in need. They are always on the lookout for causes that they can help and the audience is right there with them to donate and participate.*
>
> *Chaz and AJ are Marconi Award winners and can be heard all over the state on 99.1 WPLR and 95.9 The FOX, throughout Connecticut.*

Note: For in-depth interviews of Chaz and AJ, please see the appendix.

Ashley Gee

My favorite part of the job was connecting with Connecticut's "Tribe Members," the name fondly given to fans of WPLR.

—*Ashley Gee*

Ashley Gee was born and raised in Connecticut. She started listening to WPLR in high school and became an avid fan throughout college and graduate school. As Ashley put it, "College and graduate school were both out of state, so listening to PLR was a way for me to bring a tiny piece of home with me."

When she returned to Connecticut, she continued to listen to WPLR. One day, Ashley heard of a job opening at PLR over the air. Despite little on-air experience, Ashley was determined. As she explained, "I pursued the job opening single-mindedly and without hesitation. I landed the job with only amateur experience at a radio station on my college campus."

Ashley Gee, WPLR. *Courtesy of Ashley Gee.*

Ashley Gee became a popular on-air personality when she emerged as the "third voice" of the PLR fan-favorite show *Chaz and AJ in the Morning*, which airs on WPLR from 5:30 a.m. to 10:00 a.m. She was a member of the Chaz and AJ team from 2019 to 2022. Ashley fondly recalls many occasions in which, in her own words, "I laughed until I cried…a lot." She remembers zany moments such as watching East Haven police dancing awkwardly to a Taylor Swift song after losing a bet, playing iPod-O-Rama (attempting to name songs/artists faster than other show members) and "sharing intimate, zany details of my personal life with PLR listeners (including my engagement and my wedding)."

Her other roles on the show consisted of guest coordinator and traffic reporter.

As the guest coordinator, Ashley booked a wide variety of celebrities, rock stars, comedians, professional athletes and authors. She also booked a diverse assortment of experts in fields such as travel, movies, dating, automotive, paranormal and more. Ashley said, "The variety of very talented guests was impressive and should serve as proof that there are amazing people all around us here in Connecticut."

Her role as guest coordinator took on a new meaning once the COVID-19 pandemic hit. Ashley reflected on that period of time working at WPLR:

> *I was in my role for less than a year when the COVID-19 pandemic started. As the guest coordinator, it was my responsibility to track down knowledgeable doctors, hairdressers and grocery store employees that could give advice and shed light on current events in Connecticut. The morning show, which is defined as a comedy show, ultimately decided to focus on more than the news. We tried to find "the funny" in everyday life. The show was extended by an hour during the height of the pandemic, and by focusing on lighter topics and laughing as much as possible, we hoped to engage Connecticut's community in a way that would create an escape from the world's uncertainty.*

While at WPLR, Ashley Gee was the on-air host of *Nights with Ashley* from 2020 to 2022. Her show aired on PLR from 7:00 p.m. until midnight, Ashley reflected on her listening audience while working at WPLR:

> *I was always touched at how PLR's audience truly listened and paid attention to small details. For example, at a Halloween party, at least a dozen or more of our station's loyal listeners had made a point to bring*

my favorite alcohol—Fireball. There was no need for me to hit the bar at that event.

I spent nearly four years striving to make people laugh over the air, which came in a variety of wacky forms, including: eating gross food, playing games, singing karaoke (badly) or trying to break open a watermelon by squeezing it between my legs (unsuccessfully).

My favorite part of the job was connecting with Connecticut's "Tribe Members," the name fondly given to fans of the station. These people were like me. They were the people who I grew up with, the people who supported me and the people who I believe in.

18

WNAB

WNAB Background

WNAB 1450 was located on Broad Street in Bridgeport, Connecticut. At one point, WNAB's slogan was "We're Nuts About Bridgeport" to coincide with the station's call letters. In 1985, WNAB left the air, and radio station WJBX took over as an "oldies" station. The channel then became Spanish radio station Radio Cumbre in 1989.

Notable WNAB On-Air Personalities

Wildman Steve Gallon

In 1961, famed disc jockey/promoter "Wildman" Steve Gallon produced a big show at the New Haven Arena starring Brook Benton, the Shirelles, Dave "Baby" Cortez and Little Anthony and the Imperials. The show was sold out, and each act received a great reaction from fans.

There was a lot of Connecticut pride on the line as that concert also featured a Battle of the Bands contest featuring Connecticut bands: the Five Satins, the Nutmegs and Roger Koob and the Premiers. So there was some serious talent in that room when you think of Fred Parris (Five Satins), Leroy Griffen (Nutmegs) and Roger Koob (Premiers).

New Haven (and Connecticut) had a lot to be proud of that night.
—Bill Koob of the Premiers

Steve Gallon (born September 10, 1925) is one of the pioneers of Top 40 radio. He attended school in Waterbury, Connecticut, and began his radio career at Waterbury's WATR. He became known as "Wildman Steve Gallon."

After WATR, Wildman worked at Bridgeport's WNAB from 1959 to 1961.

Aside from working as a disc jockey, Wildman Steve found success as a comedian and promoter. In 1970. Steve released a comedy album titled *My Man! Wild Man!*

Harry Luke

Harry Luke Lukachik (a.k.a. Harry Luke) was a graduate of Bridgeport's Harding High School and Boston College (class of 1943).

In 1954, Harry joined the on-air staff at Bridgeport's WNAB, where he was appointed program director and was known for his afternoon show *Swing Angel*, a music and quiz show. Prior to WNAB, Harry worked at Bridgeport's WICC radio station.

Opposite, top to bottom: Chuck Berry, Sandy Stewart ("My Coloring Book"), Alan Freed; Alan Freed with Buddy Holly; Alan Freed with Little Richard and Bill Haley. *Courtesy of Judith Fisher Freed.*

19

TRIBUTE TO ALAN FREED

Alan Freed, who lived in Connecticut for some time, was a hero of mine. I was very fortunate and thrilled to work with Alan Freed in 1959 at WINS.

—*Ken Griffin*

One of the most popular and influential pioneers in the history of rock 'n' roll, Alan Freed gained legions of fans as a disc jockey, concert promoter, record hop emcee and film star. Freed also hosted his own Friday night ABC-TV show, which aired in July 1957, called the *Big Beat Show*. Freed resided in Stamford, Connecticut, for a time at his home known as the Greycliff Manor. There he hosted many music executives and made plans to bring rock 'n' roll to the big screen.

Alan Freed was urged by a record store owner, Leo Mintz, to host his own radio program at Cleveland's WJW radio station. It was while working at WJW that Freed coined the phrase "rock 'n' roll." His fame grew while he was at WINS and WABC radio stations in New York City, when he earned the nickname "Mr. Rock 'n' Roll."

Freed was one of the first inductees into the Rock and Roll Hall of Fame in 1986. In fact, Cleveland was chosen as the home of the Rock and Roll Hall of Fame as a tribute to Alan Freed.

Top: "Rate The Record" on Alan Freed's *Big Beat* TV show. *Left to right*: singer Jackie Wilson, singer Jimmy Clanton and Freed, others unidentified. *Courtesy of Judith Fisher Freed.*

Bottom, left: Alan Freed, WINS radio; *right*: Alan Freed, WJW radio. *Both courtesy of Judith Fisher Freed.*

ALAN FREED
Mr.Rock 'N Roll"

WINS
1010 On Your Dial

Alan Freed. *Courtesy of Judith Fisher Freed.*

20

TELEVISION DANCE SHOWS HOSTED BY CONNECTICUT DISC JOCKEYS

S everal Connecticut disc jockeys also had their own highly successful television dance shows:

Connecticut Bandstand

I was fortunate to be a member of the singing group called the Academics. We appeared in many Connecticut music venues, and the fan reaction was terrific. In 1958, we performed our fan-favorite song "Somethin' Cool" on the popular Connecticut Bandstand *TV show. As we approached the bandstand stage, the girls were screaming so loud that it was difficult to hear the intro for our song. The sound was deafening! But it was a lot of fun, and I have such good memories of that show and the other Connecticut music venues we performed in.*

—Marty Ganter of the Academics

⊙ ⊙ ⊙

The Premiers closed out 1960 with a guest appearance on the Connecticut Bandstand *New Year's Special show on WNHC-TV. Bobby "Boris" Pickett was also on the show's lineup. Of course, he did his famous "Monster Mash," which was sort of weird for a*

New Year's Eve show, but it worked out well. The Premiers did our popular songs "Pigtails Eyes of Blue" and "I Pray." A fun experience! I think that was the only New Year's Eve show that Connecticut Bandstand *ever produced.* Connecticut Bandstand *was a very popular TV dance show for teenagers, and Jim Gallant treated guests on his show in a very professional manner.*

—Bill Koob of the Premiers

I went to Connecticut Bandstand *with a bunch of my friends from Sacred Heart High School in Waterbury. We had a blast, and it was so much fun dancing and watching the performers singing on the show.*

Every once in a while we would take a quick peek at the monitor and see ourselves and the other kids while we were dancing. Our families and friends tuned in to watch us on the TV show—and of course, everything was shown in black and white!

—Paula Renzoni Crean

Connecticut disc jockey Jim Gallant (born December 24, 1930) was the first host of the popular TV show *Connecticut Bandstand*.

On July 9, 1956, Dick Clark took over as host of *American Bandstand* on WFIL-TV in Philadelphia, Pennsylvania. Later that same year (October 17, 1956), WNHC-TV in New Haven began airing *Connecticut Bandstand*. Both WFIL and WNHC were station affiliates under the Triangle Publications Radio and Television company.

Connecticut Bandstand performers. *Left*: Debbie and the Darnels on *Connecticut Bandstand*; *right*: The Academics. *Left, courtesy of Dorothy Yutenkas, lead singer of Debbie and the Darnels; right, courtesy of Marty Ganter of the Academics.*

Top, left: Ginny Arnell performing on *Connecticut Bandstand*; *right*: *Connecticut Bandstand*'s dance regulars Cookie and Charley also had a Top 10 local hit. *Left, courtesy of Ginny Arnell; right, author's collection*

Bottom: *Connecticut Bandstand*'s DJ Mike Spacek. *Courtesy of Gail Romanovich.*

Opposite: *Connecticut Bandstand* dancers. *Courtesy of Gail Romanovich.*

For the most part, *Connecticut Bandstand* mirrored Dick Clark's national *American Bandstand*. The show's format featured teenagers in and around Connecticut who danced to hit songs that were popular at the time. Local pop artists from Connecticut performed on the show, lip-syncing to their recordings. Like *American Bandstand*, the *Connecticut Bandstand* show featured dance regulars who gained local fame and even had their own fan clubs. Two such regulars were a couple known as Cookie and Charley. Cookie Teznick and Charley (Charlie) Lent were a popular dancing duo on the show in 1957. Later that year, Cookie and Charley recorded two singles—"Let's Go Rock and Roll" and "Love You So"—that were popular on a local basis, charting in the Top 20 on Connecticut radio stations. Many of the teenagers appearing on the show were students at local New Haven high schools, such as Hillhouse High and Wilbur Cross High. However, students from other high schools across Connecticut also appeared on this program.

Local recording artists that performed on Connecticut Bandstand included Debbie and the Darnels, the Catalinas, the Academics, Ginny Arnell, Andy Dio, Billy James, Roger Koob and the Premiers, the Van Dykes, the Reveliers, the Pyramids and Ron and His Rattletones.

Connecticut Bandstand aired on WNHC-TV weekdays Monday through Friday at 3:30 p.m., immediately prior to *American Bandstand.*

As previously noted, the show's first host was disc jockey Jim Gallant. He also hosted many record hops and outdoor shows featuring local performers. For example, Gallant hosted and produced concerts in 1959 at Marino's Danz-Er-Roll in Buckingham Hall in Waterbury, Connecticut. Also, it is purported that Gallant was in the running to host *American Bandstand* but the job was awarded to Dick Clark. After allegations of payola arose, Gallant resigned, refusing to sign an affidavit admitting to receiving gifts in exchange for playing records. In March 1960, Elliot "Biggie" Nevins became the show's new host. Nevins also hosted local record hops. *Connecticut Bandstand* ended in 1962 with Mike Sapack as the last host of the show.

Connecticut Bandstand was a popular TV show for viewers in and around the state.

The Brad Davis Television Dance Show

In May 1961, our song "She Gives Me Fever" reached no. 1 in New Haven and stayed that way for a while. On the strength of that song and a few other songs of ours that were popular in Connecticut, the Premiers were in demand constantly doing record hops all over Connecticut including record hops hosted by Biggie Nevins, who took over as the host of Connecticut Bandstand. *Brad Davis reached out to us and we performed on his TV dance show. It was an exciting time for us.*

—Bill Koob, member of the Premiers

The Brad Davis Show TV dance program, sponsored by the Connecticut Milk Producers Association, premiered on Hartford's WTIC-TV on October 3, 1959, and ran until 1969.

The host of the show, Brad Davis, was both a TV and radio on-air personality. The format of the show was similar to *Connecticut Bandstand,* featuring teenagers who danced to the popular tunes at the time. The show featured regional musicians and national recording artists. Brad Davis

Left: Brad Davis; *right*: Ad for appearances by Sly and the Family Stone and the Wildweeds on October 12, 1968. *Both author's collection*

hailed from Stafford Springs and graduated from Enfield High School. *The Brad Davis Show* was broadcast on WTIC-TV from 4:30 p.m. to 5:00 p.m. every Saturday.

The following are some of the artists who performed on Brad Davis's show:

SLY AND THE FAMILY STONE: Sly and the Family Stone performed on Brad Davis's TV dance show on October 12, 1968. Sly and his band were inducted into the Rock 'n' Roll Hall of Fame in 1993.

THE WILDWEEDS; Windsor's Wildweeds appeared on *The Brad Davis Show* on October 12, 1968. Sly and the Family Stone also performed on the same show

GENE PITNEY: Hall of Fame legend Gene Pitney appeared on *The Brad Davis Show* on numerous occasions. For example, Pitney performed his hit song "Town Without Pity" on the December 23, 1967 program. Also featured on the same show was the singing group the Cowsills, who performed their hit "The Rain, The Park, and Other Things."

Frankie Valli: Frankie Valli and the Four Seasons have been one of the most prolific groups in rock 'n' roll history. They were one of the few American groups to withstand the onslaught of the British Invasion. According to their website, Frankie Valli and the Four Seasons had forty songs in the Top 40, nineteen in the Top 10 and eight No. 1 hits. They also had a Top 40 hit under their alias the Wonder Who. In addition, Frankie Valli had nine Top 40 hits as a solo artist. Valli was a guest on Hartford's Brad Davis show. The original members of the Four Seasons (Frankie Valli, Bob Gaudio, Nick Massi and Tommy DeVito) were inducted into the Rock 'n' Roll Hall of Fame in 1990. The Four Seasons were also inducted into the Vocal Group Hall of Fame in 1999.

Bridge: West Haven's Bridge was best known for local hits "It's a Beautiful Day" and "Love Is There." The song "Love Is There" was a No. 1 hit on local radio (WAVZ). Much of the band's original material was written by group members Dennis D'Amato and Charley Claude. Bridge recordings took place at Trod Nossel Studios. The manager of Bridge was Art DeNicholas, the cofounder and group member of the bands the Van Dykes and the Catalinas. Bridge was popular in the New England region. The group (then known as the Symbolix) opened for the Young Rascals at the New Haven Arena. The band also performed on *The Brad Davis Show*. Bridge broke up in 1971.

Tommy and the Rivieras: West Haven's Tommy and the Rivieras was one of the groups that appeared on *The Brad Davis Show*. Fans may recall that Tommy and the Rivieras were the opening act for the Doors on December 9, 1967. During that concert, Jim Morrison of the Doors was arrested onstage and brought to the New Haven Police Department, where he was charged with obscenity and breach of peace.

The Premiers: Roger Koob and the Premiers appeared on *The Brad Davis Show* and performed some of their local hits, including "She Gives Me Fever," which was a no. 1 song in New Haven, Connecticut.

The Blue Beats: The Blue Beats were a popular garage rock band that originated in Ridgefield. Band members hailed from the Ridgefield, Danbury and Westport areas. The Blue Beats are probably best known for their rock song "Extra Girl," an extremely popular Top 10 song on Connecticut radio stations and at local dance clubs. Their follow-up recording "Born in Chicago" and its B side "I Can't Get Close (To Her at All)" were also well received in the Connecticut area. Former WDRC/WPOP disc jockey Lance Drake (radio name Scott Morgan) wrote "Extra Girl" and "I Can't Get Close (To Her at All)." The Blue Beats performed

Left: Tommy and the Rivieras; *right*: The Premiers, *left to right*: Gus Delcos, Roger Koob and Frank Polemus, with Billy Koob in the front. *Left, author's collection; right, courtesy of Bill Koob.*

on *The Brad Davis Show* and also performed as backup for major artists such as the Four Tops, Herman's Hermits at Bushnell Memorial, the Hollies at Hartford's Armory and others.

THE MIDNITE MOVERS: The Midnite Movers were an R&B/soul band from Windsor. The group was founded by Ralph DeLorso Jr. in 1968. DeLorso was a 1972 graduate of Windsor High School. The Midnite Movers appeared on *The Brad Davis Show* in 1969. The band released six songs and recorded at Syncron Studio and studios in New Haven and Hartford. After touring throughout the Northeast, the Midnite Movers disbanded in 1971.

THE UPBEATS: The Upbeats hailed from Waterbury, and the band members graduated from Waterbury's Croft High School. In 1961, Jess Evon and Ralph Calabrese formed the Upbeats. The band members consisted of Jess Evon, Ralph Calabrese, Tom Nappi and Dave San Angel. The group backed numerous nationally known artists. The Upbeats performed on *The Brad Davis Show* in 1966.

THE MARBLE COLLECTION: The Marble Collection (New Haven) appeared on *The Brad Davis Show* on two occasions.

21

DISC JOCKEY SKITS, ROUTINES AND STORIES

T he long, in-depth skits depended on the disc jockey's ability to hold the attention of an audience. These skits required a great deal of skill that some on-air personalities managed to perfect.

The WDRC "Gigantic Birds" Prank

One of the many clever promotional stunts dreamed up by WDRC program director Charlie Parker was a Thanksgiving stunt reported extensively by WDRC and its sister stations in November 1971.

On November 10, 1971, disc jockeys at WDRC and its sister stations began updating their listeners on an unusual West Coast phenomena—a large flock of beautiful, enormous multicolored birds.

At the time, Buckley Broadcasting owned WDRC. Correspondents from the news departments at Buckley's sister stations KOL Seattle (Gary West), KGIL San Fernanado (Frank Bingnam), WWTC Minneapolis (Tom O'Neill) and WIBG Philadelphia (Pete Jackson), along with WDRC on-air personalities, tracked a flock of unusual birds as they flew from the West Coast across the country until finally reaching Hartford, Connecticut, and the WDRC studio.

To give you a feel of what was involved in this prank and how it was extensively covered from Seattle to San Fernando to Minneapolis and finally to Philadelphia as reported by radio newsmen in these areas and, of course, thoroughly covered by WDRC newsmen—here is the exact reporting of this WDRC Thanksgiving hoax (as heard on 1971 radio airchecks):

Gary West (KOL Seattle) reporting:

One of the most beautiful and spectacular phenomenon of nature ever witnessed here in the Great Northwest. It all started when on a beautiful sun-splashed November day which was darkened by a sudden cloud except there were no clouds. Instead calls began to flood our KOL newsroom with excited reports that enormous flying creatures were filling the sky in a tight huge formation over the city of Seattle. The reports identified these mysterious creatures as big multicolored birds, if you can call them that, and while their appearance is frightening they made what was termed as an unbelievable beautiful sight. The birds are said to be harmless despite their size and their sound which can only be described as a weird babbling noise and which even rattled several Seattle windows. And while some Seattle residents admitted to panic and rushed into homes and gas stations, the majority stood their ground spellbound as the creatures zig-zagged in formation in the city several times before finally winging their way south.

Frank Bingman (KGIL San Fernando) reporting:

The birds arrived today in San Fernando. Not just any birds but huge creatures estimated in the area of ten to twenty pounds. They appeared unannounced in one of the most eerie sights ever seen. Calls flooded the KGIL studio with reports of gigantic babbling birds. Calmer callers referred to the giant birds as being absolutely beautiful and appeared harmless since none of them landed. It has been reported that lights needed to be turned on at a football game, not because of clouds but because of this flock of huge birds overhead.

Tom O'Neill (WWTC Minneapolis) reporting:

The birds have just appeared in Minneapolis. Traveling at an incredible speed, their first appearance was reported by a farmer, just west of Minneapolis. Having heard about these large birds, thousands of residents left their houses and cars to get a look for themselves of this strange phenomenon. The creatures were described as enormous, beautiful birds flying in close formation, flapping their huge wings and babbling loudly. Suddenly the flock flew out of sight, heading east.

Pete Jackson (WIBG Philadelphia) reporting:

> *The huge multicolored creatures have made their way to Philadelphia. The flock of birds was described as the size of a football field. Residents here say they are baffled by the mystery and the beauty of these enormous birds. Traveling at an incredible speed, the birds have just left Philadelphia. A note, just handed me, shows that it appears certain that the birds should appear over the Connecticut skies and the WDRC area shortly after four o'clock this afternoon.*

The WDRC listeners quickly caught on to this hoax and ate all of it up. They tuned in to closely follow the reporting of these "mysterious" (fictitious) birds, which was simulcast on WDRC. The Giant Bird hoax was even covered in depth by local newspapers with the headline, "Giant 'Bird' Story Shot Down As Hoax: Program by WDRC."

In actuality, this was part of a Thanksgiving turkey giveaway by the WDRC studio. But it made for good listening and a lot of fun for DRC fans.

Author's note: I hope showing the entire transcript of how this prank was carried out gives readers a sense of how radio stations and disc jockeys during the 1960s and 1970s were able to keep the attention of their listeners for long, extended periods of time. While the teenage audience caught on quickly to some of these station-orchestrated pranks, it was *how* these pranks were delivered that really made these routines a fun experience for radio listeners. Program directors like Charlie Parker and on-air personalities such as Joey Reynolds, Lee "Baby" Simms, Dick Robinson and Ken Griffin (to name a few) were geniuses at not only entertaining listeners (especially their teenage listeners) but also holding the listeners' attention for hours (and sometimes days) at a time. Routines such as this (and those that follow) would be difficult to pull off and hold listeners attention for long periods of time in today's fast-paced social media–driven environment.

Bill Stephens Recalls Two Skit Routines While at Radio Stations WDRC and WCCC

Routine 1

At WDRC in 1978, I did my evening show broadcast from a casket on Halloween night in front of JC Penny in the Westfarms Mall in

West Hartford. I was wearing a real tuxedo, wore makeup to give me an ashen complexion and was lying in a real casket borrowed from a local funeral home. To begin the night, I was wheeled into position with the lid closed before it was opened, and a microphone was placed over my mouth. Of course, my banter included numerous puns, double-entendres, death references and one-liners appropriate to the situation. "Let's not have any dead air," "Does anyone have a Hearse-ee bar?" "Hi, Bill Stephens coming to you on WDOA," etc.

Not long after the remote began, Charlie's fertile mind kicked into gear again. He came over to me and whispered, "Let's raise some money for UNICEF. Tell people they can Kiss the Corpse if they toss a Buck in the Box and the money will then go to UNICEF." I figured that was a good idea and I announced it. What happened next was extremely unexpected! Several teenage girls came over, tossed in the dollar bills and gave me very innocent kisses on my cheek. People with cameras took pictures of this (this was long before cellphones), and the crowd around the casket was getting steadily bigger. Then, several moms made their way over to me, and after dropping the money next to me, they proceeded to give me the most passionate kisses I had ever had! It was a few moments before I could say anything!

Of course, Charlie thoroughly enjoyed this spectacle, and to be honest, the moms were fairly attractive, so I did too.

Routine 2

WCCC program director Rusty Potz and I concocted a bit that became locally infamous—the "Boston Bill 35-Hour Protest." The stunt involved me playing one song, "Bitter Bad," by Melanie for thirty-five hours nonstop. The premise was I had been passed over for a full-time shift at WCCC several times and I decided to lock myself in the radio studio and play that song (and yes, it was tough to hear over and over) until the station gave me a regular gig. Rusty wanted very much to get some free publicity for the station since the owner was notoriously cheap. So to get people talking about us, we had to come up with something truly outrageous but at no cost. So, it was decided that when my shift ended at 6:00 a.m. on a certain Monday morning, as Rusty was arriving for his morning show, I would lock him out and not come out until he agreed to my demands—which included replacing him on the morning show. This was similar in concept to a stunt Joey Reynolds pulled years earlier on WPOP when he played

"Midnight Hour" by Wilson Pickett for six hours straight and also another time playing "Sherry" by the Four Seasons continuously. Not as a protest. He was just being Joey.

Over the next thirty-five hours, word of the protest spread everywhere. People began to picket outside WCCC demanding I get the morning show. I was interviewed on the phone by Don Imus and Larry Glick at WBZ in Boston, and I received a bouquet of flowers from Melanie. Stories ran in the Monday afternoon edition of the Hartford Courant *and several of the radio trade publications. Finally, at 5:00 p.m. on Tuesday, Rusty went into the news booth and announced the station management would grant my wishes and I would begin hosting mornings the next day. Rusty told me it was the greatest performance by a jock he had ever heard, which meant a lot to me.*

In my travels even until this day, I have people who know I was a Hartford DJ asking me, "Were you Boston Bill?" or "Were you the guy in Hartford who played that record for thirty-five hours?" If you go to the website Northeast Airchecks, you'll find a forty-eight-minute clip of the thirty-five-hour madness.

Steve Parker recalled one of Joey Reynolds's pranks while a disc jockey at WDRC:

At one point during his DRC shift, Joey Reynolds discovered that the record "In the Midnight Hour" was stuck in the groove. Instead of stopping the record and going onto another song, Joey allowed the recording to play on the air over and over and over again for hours. I still remember my dad, WDRC program director Charlie Parker, listening to the station in the kitchen when the police broke the studio door down. But with Joey, nothing ever surprised Dad.

Even though Joey was indeed very popular and one of the first "shock jocks" in the country, my dad finally had to fire him for calling the female mayor of Hartford a "dumb broad." Despite this, Joey and my father always remained good friends, and he's still a dear friend of mine also.

One of Ken Griffin's routines while he was at WPOP: In 1965, Ken Griffin challenged his listeners to count the records he played between 8:00 p.m. and 9 p.m. If he played fewer than twenty records per hour, the first caller would collect one hundred dollars. Twenty records in an hour!

WPOP's Woody Roberts's April Fool's stunt (1967): Woody Roberts helped orchestrate one of radio's favorite stunts, which left WPOP listeners totally confused.

On April Fool's Day 1967, the "WPOP Good Guys" traded places for the day with the on-air staff of Buffalo radio station WKBW.

And so, Stan Roberts filled in for WPOP's Bill Bland, Dan Neaverth filled POP's Danny Clayton's shoes, Jefferson Kaye became POP's Woody Roberts and Bud Ballou filled in for WPOP's Lee "Baby" Simms.

Bob Paiva (WPOP promotions director) recalled Lee "Baby" Simms and one of his on-air stunts on WPOP:

One of the fun skits pulled off by the legendary Lee "Baby" Simms went like this: Lee allegedly had a pet snake in the studio. He spent one entire show graphically describing to his on-air audience the "art" of feeding a mouse to his snake. (There was, of course, no snake.)

On a subsequent night, he claimed to have been bitten by the snake and spent the next four hours dying on-air and began pleading for help. Lee finally collapsed on the floor at the end of the show.

The following morning, Lee's best buddy Woody Roberts started his morning show with a eulogy to Lee Simms, who had "died" on the air the previous night.

As the show continued, Woody was informed that Lee did not die as he had been informed. Woody then became angry because Lee had not died and Woody wasted a perfectly good "memorial" show.

Lee informed his audience (and Woody) that a beautiful stewardess on the plane coming into Bradley Airport had heard Lee's cries for help, rushed to the WPOP studio and saved his life.

This was long-form satire taking four or more hours to execute on-air. The success of bits like this depended on the disc jockey's ability to hold the attention of an audience—and Lee was a master of doing just that!

Lee's on-air personality style was a promotion. It was inevitable that his negative comments would come back as negativity toward him personally (by some), but it was part of the design. Lee would lead the audience in the direction he planned to take them. It sounds counter to normalcy for someone to build this into their act—but Lee Simms was unique.

On another occasion, Lee was invited to address a high school class, and he asked me to accompany him for moral support. By the time we left the school, the kids loved him but the teacher hated us. The teacher had expected Lee to speak about his personal education and the value of a good education. What the teacher wanted was a pep talk. However, that would mean that Lee would have to lie, and he wasn't about to do that. Lee was deeply embarrassed by his lack of schooling, having only a sixth-grade education. In an effort to compensate, he was the only person I've ever known who actually "read" and "studied" the dictionary every day, learning new words and then attempting to use those words in conversation.

Lee was basically very shy with a withdrawn personality, plagued by his lack of formal education. His public personality was a carefully constructed façade.

Lee Simms was a unique, beloved on-air personality with a legion of fans who fondly remember "Lee Baby" even to this day.

How WPOP brought the Beach Boys to the East Coast for the first time, as told by WPOP's Bob Paiva:

One night we were sitting around at WPOP talking about acts we'd like to bring to Hartford as part of the WPOP series at the Bushnell, and somebody mentioned the Beach Boys.

At the time, the Beach Boys were a new sensation on the West Coast but had never toured the East Coast. In fact, the group had no idea how popular their music was on the East Coast.

Ken Griffin picked up the phone and called Murry Wilson, the father of the original Beach Boys and their manager at the time. Murry was actually listed in the phonebook, and he picked up the phone. He told Ken that the Beach Boys would not come east unless they had at least five dates to perform.

Ken went to work. He called Worcester's WORC, Providence's WPRO and another radio station in Albany, New York. By the end of the evening, he rounded up commitments from five stations to host a Beach Boys show.

Ken phoned those names back to Murry Wilson, and shortly after that the first East Coast Beach Boys tour was announced.

At that point, I entered the picture, as it was my job to coordinate the show at the Bushnell for WPOP.

Murry's terms were unbelievable. The Beach Boys were to get 100 percent of the ticket sales and 100 percent of all "collateral" revenue (programs, T-shirts, etc.). WPOP got nothing. Not only did we get no money, but we had to pay for the use of the Bushnell, for security and for *any other normal operating expenses. We were also limited to being able to say "WPOP Presents the Beach Boys" in our on-air spots promoting the show. Since we would not receive any revenue (that all went to Murry), we priced the tickets at $2.50 each.*

Even though we took a hit financially, being the first to get the Beach Boys to appear in concert on the East Coast was a ratings booster for our station, especially since there was such a fierce rivalry for ratings with WDRC.

In short, the first East Coast tour of the Beach Boys was the brainchild of Ken Griffin, and his many efforts to bring the group to Hartford really paid off for us.

And by the way, who knew that Murry Wilson would actually answer his phone?

WDRC Dick Heatherton stunt: In a very memorable stunt, Dick Heatherton initiated a forty-hour, seven-minute on-air marathon prank during which the other WPOP Good Guys were supposedly kidnapped. This was another stunt that depended on the disc jockey's ability to hold the attention of an audience. And it was carried out masterfully.

Marcia Win recalled her role as "Miss Fox" on WPOP:

Woody and I did the first two-person morning show in Hartford radio. At that time there were no women in Top 40 stations!

My maiden name was Fox, and so Woody jumped with that. And so, we were Woody and his secretary, "Miss Fox."

Off the air I did some basic secretarial stuff around the station. Woody and I did funny little bits a few times per hour, and we did have a great deal of fun and lots of fans!

WPOP's Bob Paiva remembered the "Woody and Miss Fox" bits very well, saying:

Miss Fox was Woody's on-air foil. Marcia Win as "Miss Fox" was marvelous!

Woody taught me that if you want people to "hear" you on the radio you need to create a disruption. Otherwise, people have the radio on but they are not "listening," especially during the morning show. People are getting out of bed, getting dressed, preparing breakfast, planning their day, getting the kids' lunches ready for school, etc. Listeners are usually doing something else while listening to the radio, so their focus may be divided unless the radio disc jockeys become interesting and the listeners stop what they are doing for the moment.

Enter "Miss Fox" and how her role enabled Woody to get people's attention.

Take, for instance, the weather forecast. Woody used Miss Fox very effectively for situations like this. Woody would announce that he was going to read the weather and then he would be heard fumbling around looking for the weather script. In frustration, he would call out in a loud voice for Miss Fox who would come to his rescue, as a loyal secretary, finding the weather forecast for him. By then he totally involved the audience into his show.

Marcia sat in the studio with Woody, and every day he would use her a number of times to draw attention to something he wanted the audience to hear and remember. He was the fumbling, incompetent "boss" and she was the loyal, efficient secretary who saved him every day.

Marcia Win as "Miss Fox" carried it off brilliantly!

Woody Roberts and Marcia Win, "Miss Fox." *Courtesy of Marcia Win.*

WDRC's "PROOF" IN 1969 that Paul McCartney had died in 1966 and that Elvis Presley died at birth: When the big commotion erupted over the claim that Paul McCartney had died in 1966 and that the Beatles album covers all had clues to prove this, WDRC did a one-hour exposé on the issue.

Taking their cue from the "McCartney is dead" rumor, Bill Winters and Danny Clayton put together their own one-hour exposé proving that Elvis had died at birth and that his twin brother, Pervis, had been impersonating him since birth. They played Elvis songs backward to prove this.

WPOP's MIKE GREENE SHARED three of his recollections while at WPOP (1968–1970):

> *Steve O'Brien used to introduce the song "Midnight Confessions" by saying: "Two priests, no waiting!"*

> *When the WPOP jocks played basketball games against high school cheerleaders, Dick Heatherton and Steve O'Brien would start looking at a random girl in the stands and start yelling "Oh my God, it's Susan!" They would stop playing and run into the stands yelling it louder and louder until they got to the poor girl and then they would shake their heads and yell, "It's not Susan!"*

> *I received a great deal of comments on the air when I introduced, for the first time, the song "I Am a Rock" when it first came out. I introduced the song as "Simon and Rock and I Am a Garfunkel."*

THE BEHIND-THE-SCENES STORY OF the Rolling Stones' arrival in Hartford for their Dillon Stadium concert and other Mick Jagger stories, as told by WPOP's Bob Paiva:

> *The Stones came to Hartford's Dillon Stadium during their 1966 American tour. I believe their song "Paint It Black" was just released. At the time, I was the WPOP music and promotions director and was made stage manager for the show since the concert was sponsored by WPOP radio.*
>
> *When I got the contract for the Stones' appearance it specified Cadillac limousines, each to contain a case of chilled Coca-Cola. I did not want to waste the station's money on Cadillac limousines so I sent a couple of "Checker" cabs to pick them up at the airport and bring them to the stadium.*

The thing I remember most about that concert was that the crowd broke loose and started to charge the stage. I immediately signaled to Mick Jagger to cut the performance short to get them off the stage before the crowd overwhelmed security. I had an ambulance standing by, and we did have to haul away one fan who tried to climb over the fence at Dillon Stadium, but that was the extent of the injuries.

I got the group off the stage, into the Checker cabs, and headed them back to the airport before the crowd reached the stage.

The City of Hartford totally overreacted, calling the event a "riot," and live, outdoor concerts, especially those at Dillon Stadium were banned for years.

The Rolling Stones in Hartford—exciting stuff!

Years later, Jerry Greenberg (president of Atlantic Records) called me and asked if I wanted to go to a Stones concert. We left Jerry's house in Wilton, Connecticut, and were driven out to a private airport on Long Island. We flew in a private jet to Pittsburgh. At the concert, I was left in my seat while Jerry and his wife went backstage at the music venue. After the concert, we were driven back to the plane where Jerry, his wife and Mick Jagger were awaiting the arrival of the pilots and me. That's how I got an hour-and-a-half private interview with Mick Jagger as we flew back to the Long Island airport. What I found fascinating about that leg of the trip was that Mick had with him the books from the concert. He was reviewing ticket sales, income from collateral sales and all other financial elements of the concert. My understanding is that Mick graduated from the London School of Economics, and I saw that training at work.

A few months later, I was on a private Warner Brothers jet with Mick Jagger and Jerry Greenberg. Once we landed at the Long Island Airport, a limo was supposed to be waiting to take Mick to Ahmet Ertegun's house in the Hamptons. When the limo failed to show up, a Warner Brothers employee (Mark) who was on the plane volunteered to drive Jagger to Ahmet's house in his VW Beetle car.

On the way to Ertegun's house, Jagger said he was hungry and wanted a burger. According to Mark, he and Mick pulled into a local Islip (New York) burger joint that was filled with fans that attended the Saturday night Demolition Derby car racing. The people in the burger joint were perplexed. Standing in line to buy a burger was this guy who looked like, dressed like and talked like Mick Jagger. But what would Mick Jagger be doing on a Saturday night in Islip, New York?

According to Mark, Jagger got such a kick out of it that they spent part of the night driving around Islip and stopped in another burger joint to buy burgers and confusing demolition derby fans. Is it possible that this was Mick Jagger? It couldn't be, could it? Curiously, Mark said that it appeared to him that the customers of these burger places didn't believe it was really Mick Jagger and didn't approach him to ask.

The whole story sounded like great fun and like something someone with a mischievous personality like Jagger might do.

WPOP disc jockey Bob Scott's stunt: In a carefully orchestrated publicity stunt, WPOP disc jockey Bob Scott locked himself inside of WPOP's studio on Sunday January 11, 1959, and played the "Children's Marching Song" for twelve hours, with the "goal" of forcing management to give him a full-time job at the station.

General manager Phil Zoppi and station manager Ken Cooper played the stunt with a straight face even when three hundred Trinity College students marched en masse to the WPOP studio demanding some other music be played. Hartford Police Department sent a number of policemen to break up the rally. The next day, the local newspaper headline read, "Trinity Students Invade Radio Studio As Same Record Is Played for 12 Hours."

The result was that Bob Scott was given a full-time job at the station, which had already been arranged.

WDRC's interview with Meatloaf, as told by WDRC on-air personality Bill "FM" Stephens:

In 1978, Meatloaf (real name Marvin Lee Aday) came to Hartford to play a concert at the Hartford Civic Center. Program director Charlie Parker arranged for "Meatloaf" to come to DRC's radio station for me to interview him. But Charlie being Charlie, just doing the typical Q & A on the air was just too normal. Meatloaf's big hit "Paradise by the Dashboard Light" was the most-requested song on DRC, so Charlie decided the station would hire a limousine, drive around Hartford with Meatloaf and me in the back, and it would be an "Interview by the Dashboard Light." It was a great idea.

While Meatloaf and I were cruising around the city doing an interview, he asked if we could stop for a Coca-Cola. We saw a Burger King up ahead, and we pulled in. When he and I walked into the building, the young customers and the workers behind the counter absolutely freaked out! We both had no idea he would be so recognized since he had not made many TV appearances up until that time, but the place blew up! We ended up staying there over a half hour as he signed autographs and talked to everyone.

A WPOP APRIL FOOL's prank as told by Bob Paiva:

One April Fools Day, WPOP surprised the audience by replacing the disc jockeys for the day.

I replaced the morning show 6:00 a.m. to 10:00 a.m. with a performer named Ronnie Dyson who had a hit record at the time and had appeared on Broadway.

10:00 a.m. to 2:00 p.m. featured Harry Chapin, who turned out to be an excellent disc jockey. He was interesting, quick-witted and handled the board as though he did it every day.

3:00 p.m. to 7:00 p.m. featured Tony Orlando, who I'd known previously. He was working for April-Blackwood Publishing but had just released the first "Tony Orlando and Dawn" single. He asked me to do the show with him. I ran the board, and Tony regaled the audience with stories.

Jim Croce was supposed to do the 7:00 p.m. to 12:00 a.m. shift, but radio wasn't his thing. He said he would not do a DJ stint but would perform live in concert for an hour. I set up the conference room as a studio, and for an hour Jim Croce, accompanied by his guitarist Murray Muleheisen, performed.

I was honored to receive a gold record for Jim's song "Bad Bad LeRoy Brown" because the first time the song was performed on the radio was during that one-hour live concert. He had not yet recorded it.

That was a fun promotion.

BOB PAIVA RECALLED AN unexpected encounter with a future rock legend:

One of our promotions on WPOP involved giving away several round-trip tickets to contest winners. I traveled to London with the station manager to set things up. As we were driving along, I saw an Aston Martin DB5 in a gasoline station and asked the cabbie to stop so I could get a good look at a "James Bond car."

While I was looking at the car, the owner came over, introduced himself and we talked. When he found out I was in radio he told me his name was Elton John and he was releasing his first U.S. single, "Lady Samantha," on the DJM record label that week. It was at the very beginning of his illustrious career. In another year or two, he would become a world-wide phenomenon.

Marcia Win ("Miss Fox" at WPOP) recollection of Joey Reynolds:

When I was a kid, I swear I was Joey Reynolds's biggest fan. Since we didn't have our driver's license yet, my girlfriend and I used to take a bus from East Hartford, Connecticut, to Buffalo to see him when he moved to Buffalo's WKBW. The bus trip took thirteen hours total. But it didn't seem to faze us since our goal was to see our idol. One time we got held over in Syracuse because of a huge snowstorm. So we spent the night in a Greyhound station. We were crazy kids. Joey and everybody we met were perfect gentlemen, though.

We actually went to see Joey several times! He took us to a recording studio, where a Buffalo group, "The Sessions," was cutting a record, and we stopped in to see his cool apartment which had an indoor swimming pool. I remember Joey taking us to a record hop in Grand Island, New York. Joey also took us to meet the Four Seasons on several occasions.

While visiting WKBW we got to meet Rod Roddy and Dan Neaverth, who worked on Joey's show.

Marcia Win (WPOP's "Miss Fox") recalled Woody Roberts:

When I first met Woody Roberts, he knew me only as Marcia. I was working as a promo girl for Trinity Record Distributors at the time. When he asked me to be on his show, he said, "I don't even know your last name!" When I said "Fox," he laughed and said, "Perfect!" I wasn't sure why, but I could almost see the wheels in his mind turning. Woody was a genius in creating radio skits and characters. It turns out that he was looking for a name for a character for an on-air radio skit he was planning. So the name "Miss Fox" fit perfectly for the character he had in mind. The routine featured a bumbling boss (Woody) and his very competent secretary (me). So, I became "Miss Fox."

I used to pick Woody up in the mornings to be on the air, then rush to my job at Trinity. I did that for about six months. When Woody asked me to work full time in his office, I quit the record promotion job and went full-time to work at WPOP.

Also, Woody drove a Corvette, and being a Texas boy, he didn't want to drive in the winter. Woody and I had lunch every day at the nearby Red Coach Grill.

Lee "Baby" Simms was our evening on-air personality. Lee was a very sweet person. Very shy and I liked Lee a lot. Gary Girard was overnights, Danny Clayton mid-days, then Bill Winters worked the afternoon drive. I eventually became Mrs. Bill Winters (up until his death in 1975). Our daughter, Grahame Winters was a Program Director at WDRC for a number of years. Grahame still does voice tracks for Koffee FM in Cape Cod. She is married to "Slater" at WCCC-FM. We are a radio family.

Woody Roberts, Halloween 1967. *Courtesy of Marcia Win.*

Looking back on my WPOP days and working with Woody, I can honestly say that we had sooo much fun! I loved Woody and miss him dearly!

Incidentally, even after he left the station in 1968, Woody Roberts continued to call me Fox, right up until he passed away in May 2023.

WDRC's LONG JOHN WADE, Aaron Shepard and Ron Landry with the Beatles: Upon his return from visiting with the Beatles in 1965, Long John Wade was left with a special souvenir—a caricature of "Long John" drawn by Paul McCartney.

WDRC's Long John Wade became close friends with the Beatles, in particular Paul McCartney and John Lennon. In August 1964, Charlie Parker sent him on the Beatles' American tour for several weeks, during which he sent back live reports.

In February 1965, Long John vacationed with the Beatles in Nassau, and he was with them at the Warwick Hotel in New York for their famous press conference on August 13, 1965.

WDRC's Aaron Shephard and Ron Landry also interviewed the Beatles.

DANNY LYONS, "THE STRANGER": While at radio station WKCI (aka KC101), on-air personality Danny Lyons began a regular routine known as "Soap Opera Updates." After playing the song "Rise" by Herb Albert, Danny was informed that this tune was featured in the enormously popular *General Hospital* soap opera, featuring soap opera's first "supercouple"—Luke and Laura (Spencer). Luke and Laura (and their TV wedding) were extremely popular at that time. Based on feedback from his listening audience, Lyons decided to include in his program a regular routine that he called "Soap Opera Updates." The routine proved to be highly successful with radio station listeners.

In December 1982, Danny actually appeared in an episode of the TV soap opera *One Life to Live*. In that episode, he played the part of Aaron Caplan. Danny's character in the storyline was referred to as "The Stranger."

BRIAN SMITH (WPLR AND WOW radio) recalled a WPLR Smith and Barber stunt and also shares a couple of broadcasts he was involved in:

> *While working at WPLR, one of my favorite bits involved a turkey giveaway for Thanksgiving. Unbeknownst to the winner, they were live turkeys. Our road crew went to a convenience store and asked a very simple question to the owner, with the promise of a prize of a turkey for Thanksgiving. The owner answered correctly, of course, and expected a frozen turkey. Instead, our crew pushed a live turkey into the store and "accidentally" left a cell phone (with speaker on) inside on the counter. This allowed us to "accidentally" listen to the hilarious results. The owner of the store panicked. He tried in vain to get the obviously unhappy turkey out the door of his store. But our crew eventually guided the turkey out of the convenience store and helped clean up the feathers and toppled displays.*
>
> *Also, while at WPLR, Rodney Dangerfield had Bruce Barber and I removed from opening his show at the Palace Theater in New Haven because we got a rousing applause when we walked out on stage to introduce him. Rodney didn't like us taking the attention away from him.*
>
> *I once narrated a series of syndicated short broadcasts for airplay in countries in Asia. One broadcast for China highlighted Louis' Lunch in New Haven, the reputed originator of the "hamburger." Also, a broadcast for Japan highlighted the New Haven, Connecticut music roots of the legendary group the Carpenters.*
>
> *I remember in 1993, calling the first pitch of the now defunct New Haven Ravens baseball team, and in 2011, I was the on-field promotional*

announcer and entertainer for the Bridgeport Bluefish baseball team. During the winter months, I provided a similar role for the Fairfield University basketball teams.

Finally, I narrated the documentary Last Days of the Coliseum, *which detailed the creation and the demolition of the New Haven Coliseum, an iconic Connecticut sports and entertainment facility.*

Memories of Famed WDRC Program Director Charlie Parker

After his service in the navy ended, Charlie Parker began to look for work. One day, he went to 750 Main Street in Hartford and asked for a tour of WDRC's facilities. The receptionist who showed him around was Anne M. Welch, who also did part-time announcing on an afternoon "advice-type" show.

Steve Parker and Kathy (Parker) Morgan shared their insightful memories about growing up as children of famed WDRC program director Charlie Parker and his wife, Patty. This August 2007 posting is used with permission from Ed Brouder, webmaster of his outstanding WDRC site.

> *Kathy: I have fond memories of visiting my dad's WDRC office as a very little girl. He would take me to the station's music library and find duplicate records, saying "Would you like to have these records to listen to at home?" It was about then the I started to realize that my dad's job was a lot more fun than most of my friends' fathers.*

Anne was known on-air as "Patty," a name she earned because her ready sense of humor meant she often giggled. A fellow staff member called her a "Silly Patty," and the nickname stuck. Charlie and Patty were instantly attracted to one another and began dating.

On June 7, 1945, WDRC announcer Larry Colton announced Patty and Charlie's engagement during his afternoon *Music Off the Record* program. The two were married on October 20. Charlie's best man was station announcer Dean Luce.

Mr. and Mrs. Parker continued to work at WDRC for several years and settled in Newington. Daughter Kathy was born in 1952, and Steve followed in 1955.

Around 1958, Charlie was promoted from production manager to program manager. Charlie had a great sense of humor. He kept a statue of Jack Benny in his office. If Charlie was at odds with management, Jack Benny would be facing the wall when you went into the office. If everything was OK, you saw Jack facing in toward you.

Charlie was at the helm as WDRC began divorcing itself from the CBS Radio Network, instituting a personality-driven, popular music format.

Patty Parker was only forty-three when she died of a heart attack on February 19, 1964, Kathy was eleven, and Steve was eight years old. It was right after the Beatles had caused such a huge sensation on the Ed Sullivan show—and it was at the height of WDRC's success.

Steve: The radio station was our life support at that particular time. We got really, really lifted and it brought us into the world of radio fun at the same time Mom was leaving us. The radio station was like family. It wasn't easy, but our dad vowed to keep his family together and he made a point of involving Kathy and me in the radio station.

Steve: My dad used to take Kathy and I and we'd go on radio "listening" trips. It might just be down to Waterbury, or Springfield. Once we went on a weeklong trip throughout New England and stayed in hotels.

Kathy: And we had to be quiet in the car. We'd drive and drive and we could talk during the songs but the minute the disc jockey came back on... SSSHHH...and he'd turn it up and we would just drive around listening to all these different voices.

Steve: He would listen to every disc jockey's "aircheck" that came in. He'd work on the desk, and I was on the reel-to-reel and would put on all the airchecks that came in.

Kathy: Dad brought the airchecks home, too. He played them for us quite often. I was a real fan of Dick McDonough, the quality of his voice. I think it was the voice quality he looked for.

Steve: There was a certain warmth and "richness" that he looked for. There really was a certain Big D sound. Some guys could really be good, but they just didn't have the Big D sound.

Kathy: Steve and I soon became station insiders. We were privy to a lot of secrets. The first couple of WDRC "Secret Sounds" were done at our house. One of them was the sound of roller skates, capturing me skating up and down the sidewalk in front of our house. I also remember Dad bringing home a stack of new pop records and playing them with Steve. I'd be trying to study and I was, like, "Dad, can you turn down the music?" He was very creative, crazy creative—always making everything fun.

Kathy: Some of our fondest memories were of attending Big D Big Shows at the Bushnell Memorial with our dad. When my dad emceed all those shows we were still very young so he also had to keep an eye on us. So, the majority of the time we would be backstage with him. Sometimes he would put us in the orchestra pit, but very rarely did we sit in the audience.

I was about ten years old when my dad brought us to a Big D show that featured pop artist Diane Renay. Dad said, 'You're going to have to be really, really good and very polite." I remember Diane was very, very tiny. She was only seventeen at the time. Blonde, she wore this navy outfit. And she had all this makeup on and all this hair. I'd never seen a person that looked like that. So we watched her perform very close by, singing her hit tune "Navy Blue," which reached number six on Billboard.

Kathy: The performers used to do two shows. We usually ate with whoever was performing. The one artist I remember being so kind to us, absolutely without a doubt, was Cher. Cher spent a tremendous amount of time—most of her break between the two shows—sitting there eating and talking with us.

Kathy: Steve and I remember very well the commotion caused by Bobby Rydell, who was one of the top performers in the U.S. at the time. Bobby was performing way out at the end of the stage and at one point a whole bunch of girls just vaulted up onto the stage. That was it. He dropped the microphone, and he started running while the girls were still grabbing on to him. He was cut, he was bleeding, and his ring was stolen. So I grabbed Steve. We were about to get trampled. My dad went with Bobby, and he turned to me and he yelled, "Hang on to your brother!" They went out the back door straight into a limo. I didn't know what to do. I had Steve by the hand and I'm going, "Dad!?" I was probably ten or eleven, and Steve was about seven or eight years old.

Kathy: There were times when Dad's responsibilities prevented him from coming home at night, like during the Great Northeast Blackout in November 1965. He slept on the conference room table that night. There was never a doubt in our minds that no matter what was going on over there, he was going to take care of things and at the same time, make sure we were taken care of first and foremost.

Kathy: Dad sometimes would bring home vinyl 45s for us, because we got to be old enough for him to get our opinions. That was pretty interesting. I remember one in particular. He let me hear Bobby Goldsboro's new song

"Honey" (which turned out to become a major hit record). My dad said, "Kathy, I think this would be a good one for you to listen to. I really need your opinion on this one." I remember just bawling my eyes out—"oh, it's so wonderful!"

Steve: And there were other perks, like the time that WDRC's music director Bertha Porter invited our family to a Beatles concert. She's the one that got tickets for us to see the Beatles. It was my dad, Bertha, Kathy and me in Shea Stadium, in 1966. My dad always said that the success of the station was Bertha. She knew how to pick the music!

Steve: Kathy and I grew up considering the WDRC on-air personalities as our big brothers. I don't remember anyone who was higher up the list as far as who Dad liked. I really don't. He liked them all. He knew how to work with on-air personalities and earn their trust. You don't direct a Joey Reynolds the same way you're going to direct a Sandy Beach. He could bring out the devilish side of Joey Reynolds, better than Joey could.

Kathy: The other thing that I loved was when he gave the guys their on-air radio names. He renamed Donald Pesola "Sandy Beach." I found that hysterical—I was like, YES! Sandy didn't like it very much. But I loved the nickname Sandy Beach.

Steve: Dad put the "Diamond" in Diamond Jim (Nettleton's) name. He also nicknamed John Wade "Big D Wade" and then changed it to "Long John Wade." He also transformed Kenneth Sasso into "Bradley Field." And when Jack Tupper came down from Maine to host WDRC's wakeup show in 1975, my dad renamed him "Jack Morgan" as an inside tribute to his son-in-law (Kathy's husband).

Steve: I had an opportunity for an on-air gig at KISS FM in the mid-1980s. I couldn't wait to tell my dad, and I said to him, "What should I use for a radio name?" He looked at me and said, "I gave it to you when you were born!"

Steve: When Dad had to fire somebody, it was always wrenching for him. They were all like extended family. Except the night Joe Hager decided to just play King Crimson—all night!. That was bad. He didn't answer the Hotline either...that was really bad.

Kathy: Our house in Newington was not far from the Cedar Street studios and transmitter of WDRC's rival, WPOP. There was a fierce rivalry between WDRC and WPOP. Our friends who knew where our dad worked would sometimes say things like, "WPOP did something really cool last night." And I'd be like, "No they didn't!" It was such a fierce competition.

Kathy: As we grew older, we had the chance to work at WDRC. For example, Dad recruited Steve and me for the "Mystery Phone" contest, which involved identifying the number from a public phone booth. I was assigned the task of handling the public phone booth near the old Newington Theater. Dad said, "Every time I run this contest I'm going to call you and you're going to have to get to that phone." When the phone rang, I had to calmly read a pre-prepared script and get the caller's phone number so a return verification call could be made. Steve handled the public phone at the Witonbury Mall in Bloomfield.

Steve: I have to admit that I was the one who accidently put an end to Big D's famed dune buggy, named "Little Dee." I pretty much destroyed it in the family driveway while Dad was inside the house. I tried to adjust the driver's seat and accidentally crushed some wires, which shorted out, setting the dune buggy on fire.

Steve: Dad had a lot of opportunities, especially after he became Program Director of the year in 1975 from Billboard *magazine. He was constantly getting requests....You know, everybody wanted him to go to work everywhere else. He really never wanted to shake up our world.*

Kathy: Dad didn't want to move us. And he always kept our mom alive in our minds. He even had an opportunity to go to work for the Beach Boys at one point. But instead, he spent thirty-nine years working at WDRC in the state where he was born and had lived in all his life.

NOTE: STEVE PARKER IS the on-air host of WTIC's Saturday morning show beginning at 5:30 a.m. Steve features news, sports, *Traffic & Weather Together on the 8's* and interviews with a variety of news makers.

22

CONNECTICUT DISC JOCKEY AND RADIO STATION RECORDINGS

WDRC Disc Jockey Recordings

In 1961, Ron Landry as the Incognitos recorded "Dee Jay's Delemna." Side B is "Forget It" by the Incognitos.

In 1964, Dick Robinson (and the Nite Niks) recorded "Beatnik DJ." Side B is "Give Me Love" by Tommy Dae and the Nite Niks, Note: The Nite Niks were actually Rockville's Tommy Dae and the High Tensions. The High Tensions (a.k.a. Tensionettes) consisted of Annette Lettendre and Linda Draus (Tommy's sister). Both sides of this recording were written by Dick Robinson and Tommy Dae (real name Frank Draus Jr.).

In 1965, Dick Robinson (with the High Tensions) recorded "Fraze Kraze" (also known as "Fraze Craze"), after a popular phone-in feature on his show. Side B is a tune by the Tensionettes called "He's The Boy I Love." Note: Dick Robinson and Tommy Dae wrote both sides of this recording.

In 1967, WDRC produced an album called *Color Me OBG*, which was a compilation of hit songs by various artists.

WPOP Disc Jockey Recordings

In 1963 (while at WKBW), Joey Reynolds released "Rats in My Room Pt 1." Side B is "Rats in My Room Pt 2." Note: Both sides were written by Joey Reynolds and former WKBW disc jockey Danny Neaverth. In the same year, Joey recorded "Underground Surfers." Side B is "I Got Rid of the Rats."

WDRC's *Color Me OBG* album released in April 1967. *Pictured here are, from left to right:* unidentified, Don Wade, Dick Robinson, Mike Millard, Ken Griffin and Sandy Beach. *Courtesy of Ed Brouder.*

In 1964, Ken Griffin as "Ken Hartford" recorded "Jay Walker." Side B is "Little Joe Golightly" by Ken Hartford with Fats and Rocky.

In 1965 (prior to arriving at WPOP), Joey Reynolds recorded "Ma Bell You're Swell." Side B is "Rats in My Room." Note: In the 1960s, Frankie Valli and the Four Seasons recorded Joey Reynolds's theme song.

In December 1966, Joey Reynolds released "Santa's Got a Brand New Bag." Side B is "Rats in My Room."

WCCC Record Album

In 2006, Hartford's WCCC released the album *The Rock 106.9 WCCC Live At Planet Of Sound 2*, which is a compilation of songs by various recording artists.

WTIC Record Album

On November 27, 1961, radio station WTIC released the album called *The Broadcaster*, which was a symphonic tribute album composed by Robert Maxwell, former harpist with the WTIC orchestra. Note: Robert Maxwell was the famed composer of the hit songs "Ebb Tide" and "Shangri-La."

WKCI (KC-101) Record

In 1981, KC-101's Chris Evans recorded and composed a novelty recording by Hozay Smith, who was a fictional character voiced by Chris Evans. Side A of the record is "I'll Be Stoned for Christmas." Side B is "(Soon I'll Be) Out in the Cold." The song was recorded on the Fogarea label. Fogarea was a fictional town used in Chris Evans's radio bits, and "Hozay Smith" was the corrupt mayor of Fogarea.

Appendix

INTERVIEWS

Danny Lyons (Disc Jockey at Radio Station WEBE), August 25, 2023

There is a bond, not only as a radio disc jockey, but as a person. It is very rewarding to have a listener come up and say they enjoyed listening to me for so many years. Truly amazing and something I cherish.

—Danny Lyons

TR   Thank you for agreeing to this interview, Danny.

DL   My pleasure, Tony.

TR   Let's start at the beginning.

DL   Sounds good.

TR   Where were you born and raised?

DL   I was born and raised in Waterbury, Connecticut.

TR   What schools did you attend?

DL   I attended St. Lucy's Grammar School and graduated from Holy Cross High School. Both schools were in Waterbury.

TR   When in school, did you have any on-air experience on school radio?

DL   While at Holy Cross High School, one of my teachers recognized my dream to be on the radio and asked me to be the master of ceremonies for the school band concerts. He also allowed me to do school announcements over the PA system in the morning. Basically, anywhere where there was a microphone, that's where I wanted to be.

TR   Growing up, what radio stations did you listen to?

DL   My favorite radio station growing up in Waterbury was WWCO.

TR   Growing up, who were your favorite disc jockeys?

DL   I grew up listening to WWCO, hearing all those great radio personalities. My favorite radio disc jockeys at that time were WWCO's Tom Collins and the Mad Hatter. Listening to both of these on-air personalities really inspired me to want to get into the radio business myself. They made it look so easy! It seemed like so much fun playing songs and talking about the popular music at the time.

TR   After graduating from Holy Cross High School, what did you do next?

DL   I decided to take a year off to pursue a career in radio. So, I went to Florida with the intention of hitchhiking all the way up the East Coast, looking for work on one of the radio stations along the way. I must have hit every radio station in Florida until I got to West Palm Beach.

TR   What was your first radio on-air job?

DL   Well, while in Florida, I auditioned for a small country radio station in West Palm Beach owned by the great Sam Phillips. I was hired, and I started there as a radio disc jockey on September 23, 1972, my eighteenth birthday. A most exciting birthday gift!

TR   When did you begin as an on-line personality at WWCO?

DL   With two years under my belt as a radio disc jockey, I was hired as an on-air personality at WWCO in 1974. I was so fortunate that I got to work with Joe Cipriano ("Tom Collins") and then with the Mad Hatter. Both became really good friends. I spent four years at my dream job at WWCO, doing a lot of live remotes and appearances. I also did lots of charity work, spearheading huge bike-a-thons for the American Cancer Society and fundraisers for muscular dystrophy, all at the McDonald's in Waterbury. Just so much fun for such worthy causes!

TR   Following WWCO, what were your next radio jobs?

DL   After WWCO, I worked at radio station WAVZ-AM in New Haven, Connecticut. The program director at the time was Pete Stone (a.k.a. Pete Salant). As FM radio became more popular, Pete shifted the station's music format to sister FM station WKCI. And so, in 1979, WKCI was born and became an instant success. WKCI is more widely known as KC101.

TR How did you get involved in your on-air soap opera updates?

DL It was by accident—literally! [*Laughter.*] While roller skating at a roller rink on Thomaston Avenue in Waterbury, I was involved in an accident on the rink when I fell and broke my arm. So, I had to have people come into the studio to put records on the turntable for me. One time, as I was playing the song "Rise" by Herb Albert, one of the girls in the studio yelled out, "Hey, that's the song that was playing on *General Hospital* during one of the Luke and Laura episodes!" I should note that the Luke and Laura characters on the *General Hospital* soap opera were extremely popular. They became soap's first "supercouple." Their marriage as Luke and Laura Spencer was treated on TV as *the* event. Luke and Laura's "wedding" was watched by thirty million viewers and remains the highest-rated hour in American soap opera history It got me thinking. And so, every time I played "Rise" on the radio, I would give a little synopsis of what happened on the soap opera. Because so many listeners got so excited hearing me talking about a soap opera, it became a regular feature on my show. That's how "Soap Opera Updates" got started. I eventually added other shows. I actually got to appear on an episode of the *One Life to Live* soap opera. It was called an "under five" guest appearance (less than five lines). In the episode, my character was known as "The Stranger."

TR I believe you also worked at Hartford's radio station WTIC?

DL Yes. While working at KC101, I was offered a job at New York's WNBC. I worked part-time at WNBC for four years. I then worked as a radio disc jockey at WTIC, where I worked for another four years.

TR When did you begin working at WEBE?

DL When I was working at KC101, the station's program director was Curt Hansen. In 1984, Curt co-founded and launched radio station WEBE 108, which rapidly became the number one–rated radio station in Connecticut's Fairfield County and in New Haven. In March 1987, Curt hired me to do WEBE's on-air midday shift. I have been at WEBE ever since.

TR That's thirty-seven years at one radio station! That doesn't happen for many disc jockeys at radio stations.

DL Yes, I know. I feel blessed. I have a love for this radio station and for all the people who have come through and have worked here. And, of course, for our wonderful and loyal listening audience.

TR What makes WEBE a great station?

DL   I believe WEBE is special because we have always sincerely cared about our audience and the community we serve throughout the years. We have had huge contests and giveaways, and the station has supported so many charities. But mainly it's about our huge audience, which we love and never take for granted.

TR   You have been involved in several charities. Could you tell me a bit about them?

DL   Sure. I have a foundation called a Christmas Wish Foundation in which we grant wishes for people who are struggling around the holidays. The Ronald McDonald house in New Haven is another one of my favorite charities that I have cherished and done as much fundraising as I can for thirty-something years.

TR   How would you describe the role of the radio disc jockey? What is the importance of the radio disc jockey in music history?

DL   Radio disc jockeys present music to their listening audience. Beyond that, we provide happiness, give comfort and share life experiences that our listening family can identify with. There is this companionship that exists. To me, radio is a one-on-one experience, talking to one person at a time, and that's the key to communication.

TR   Being in radio for a long time, you must appeal to different generations.

DL   After spending most of my life in radio, over fifty-one years, I constantly have "generation listeners" coming up to me. They sometimes remind me of something I said that affected them in some way. It could be some advice or comfort I gave to them as parents when their children were small. Now those children have grown and become listeners themselves. And there is still a bond, not only as a radio disc jockey but also as a person. It is very rewarding to have a listener come up and say they've enjoyed listening to me for so many years. Truly amazing and something I cherish.

TR   Thank you, Danny.

DL   My pleasure. Thank you, Tony, for including me in this book.

Interview with Chaz of the *Chaz and AJ Morning Show* on WPLR, September 14, 2023

AJ came up to me, we shook hands, and he told me that he knew I wasn't responsible for his firing. He told me he was a big fan of mine when I was at PLR. I thought to myself, "What a classy thing to do, he's such a cool guy!" This is such a perfect AJ story because that's AJ—period!

TR   Chaz, congratulations on your outstanding career!

Chaz Thank you, Tony, I appreciate it.

TR   Okay, let's start from the beginning.

TR   Where were you born and raised?

Chaz I was born in Derby and raised in Shelton, Connecticut.

TR   What schools did you attend?

Chaz I attended Elizabeth Shelton Elementary and went to Shelton Intermediate School. I attended Shelton High School for three days, and then I dropped out. I was a juvenile delinquent until the system gave up on me and got tired of chasing me. My home and school life was a mess at the time. I knew I was never going to college. I kind of already discovered radio, and school just wasn't interesting for me. I did go back and got my GED.

TR   What was your first memory of on-air broadcasting?

Chaz My first memory of media in general was when I was four or five. I walked up to our black-and-white TV console in our living room and started talking to the CBS news anchor Walter Cronkite. My mother said, "He can't hear you; you can only hear him." And I thought, "That's interesting, I like that idea." So that was my first memory of thinking that broadcasting was cool.

TR   What was the first radio station that you listened to? Who were your favorite on-air personalities at the time?

Chaz Growing up, I began listening to WPLR. I would listen to Marcia Simon in the morning, Gordon Weingarth midday, Eddie Wazoo afternoon, Stoneman 6:00 to 10:00 p.m. and "Doc Rock" Bob Nary 10:00 p.m. to 2:00 am. For me, that's the classic lineup for PLR. Meeting these on-air celebrities later in life was just a mind-blowing experience for me. It was like meeting Mickey Mantle!

TR   How and when did you first become interested in radio broadcasting?

Chaz When I was a kid, my dad bought me a guitar. I tried playing guitar but found it very difficult and I stopped. But I soon found another use for the guitar amp and the microphone. I would speak into the mic, pretending I was Stoneman [*laughter*] and annoy my neighbors.

My first real dabble into radio broadcasting was when I was eleven or twelve. My friend Don and I went camping with my dad and some family members. There was absolutely nothing to do, and we were bored out of our minds. So we took our cassette and mic and pretended to be play-by-play announcers for a horseshoe tournament [*laughter*]. We made up commercials and everything. So we brought the cassette back to the campsite and played it for some of my family members. When they began laughing at some of the stuff we recorded, I was a bit intrigued by their reaction. I thought to myself, "Hmm, this is interesting." So, my friend and I began to make more cassette tapes, pretending to be radio announcers and TV announcers.

Then, one summer, I signed up for a summer work program for underprivileged children. There were a bunch of different categories to choose from. I noticed landscaping and thought, "Great I'd be outside, get a tan, and work with my hands." My family was in construction, my dad and brother were in construction, so maybe this was for me. But then I saw the category "Learn Basic Radio Skills" and thought, "Wow, could you imagine?" So Don and I signed up for that. We went to a radio station in Derby (WLNV). It was a ten-watt radio station that wasn't even on the air yet. I remember the very first day, walking into the control room and seeing the control board. I knew immediately that this was my ticket out of poverty. I was thirteen years old (1977), and I knew this was something I would want to do for the rest of my life. For me, there was no looking back.

TR What were your first on-air radio experiences?

Chaz I got my own show on that radio station in Derby that Don and I signed up for. I was infatuated with Top 40 programming and called myself "Charlie Faze" [*laughter*], and I would talk like this [imitates a Top 40 radio disc jockey]. I evolved into a rock disc jockey and then more talk with rock. I then went from WLNV to being a DJ at weddings and private parties. I worked for some time at radio station WMNR in Monroe as basically a board operator and would run other people's programs.

I then went to WYBC, which was a breeding ground for radio station WPLR. A lot of the big radio personalities in the 1970s "cut their teeth" at WYBC—on-air personalities such as Rick Allison, Bob Caron and the list goes on and on. So I did some time at WYBC. I actually got fired mid-show. The program manager actually said to me, "I hope you know this is your last show," and then he closed the door. And I thought to myself, "What an a-hole! He could have told me that *after* I was off the air, but he just wanted to make a big scene" [*laughter*]. Needless to say, we had a lot of fun during the last two hours of that show.

TR   How and when did you become involved with WPLR?

Chaz In May 1986, I filled out an intern application at WPLR. I got the call and became an intern at PLR. It took me about a year to get on the air, running the board and working part-time.

TR   What was your first show on WPLR?

Chaz I did a show at night called *Camp Overnight*. In 1990, I was promoted to the night shift. It's funny because I have all these letters in which I was written up for doing bad things on the *Camp Overnight* show [*laughter*]. It was, like, every month I was getting written up. But then the next month I got promoted [*laughter*]. So I thought, "Well, this is pretty cool."

TR   When did *Camp Chaos* air?

Chaz I did *Camp Chaos* on WPLR from 1990 until 1994.

TR   What happened after *Camp Chaos*?

Chaz In 1994, I went from the night shift in New Haven to mornings in Dallas and forty other radio markets on the Z-Rock network, which was part of the ABC network in Dallas. I was there for a year, and the ratings were awesome! Management actually loved me. However, Disney began purchasing ABC. As it was happening, I did a bit which got the attention of one of the radio stations in the "Bible Belt" and they wrote a letter to Disney management. It became a big deal. My show briefly jeopardized the $30 billion radio/television purchase, which was, at the time, the biggest media purchase on the planet [*laughter*]. I heard that Disney management called my boss's boss's boss and asked, "Who is this a-hole?" [*laughter*]. And that was the end of my time there. Actually, they were so great about letting me go saying, "Sorry, we love you, but this is business." Which I understood.

TR   Where did you go after your time in Dallas?

Chaz From Dallas, I went back to WPLR on a part-time basis for a little while, sending out airchecks and mailing out tapes to everywhere. From there I went to California for three months.

TR   Tell me about your experience working at WRCN and what happened there.

Chaz   After California, I was hired by WRCN on Long Island. At the time
        they hired me, the morning show host was my now radio partner of
        twenty-six years (AJ). So they fired AJ and hired me. And that was
        awkward. I listened to AJ on a Friday doing his last show, knowing
        that he was not aware that it was his last show. That's the tough part
        of the business. So they fire him and I come in to do the mornings.
        A couple of weeks later, I did an event at a bar where he was a DJ.
        AJ came up to me, we shook hands and he told me that he knew I
        wasn't responsible for his firing at WRCN. He told me he was a big
        fan of mine when I was at PLR. I thought to myself, "What a classy
        thing to do, he's such a cool guy!" This is such a perfect AJ story
        because that's AJ—period! WRCN eventually hired AJ back to do
        the night show. I was then hired to be the station's program director.
        I listened to AJ at night and thought he's okay. However, when we
        had our staff meetings, he had everyone rolling in laughter. He was
        just hysterical! It occurred to me that he's the guy at the back of
        the bus, not the driver. So I moved AJ from nights into the morning
        show with me—and that was the greatest decision I ever made in
        my career! We've been together for (well, we're not good at math)
        but I believe it is twenty years at PLR and six years before that.
        And we were tearing it up on WRCN, beating everybody, beating
        Howard Stern, beating the big radio stations, and we started to get
        big radio interviews.

TR   During your time at WRCN, did you ever hear from WPLR?

Chaz   Yes. While this was all happening, we get a call from WPLR. My good
        friend Eddie Sab, who I interned with in 1986, was now program
        director and told me he didn't know what's happening with Smith
        and Barber. He asked me if AJ and I were interested in taking over
        the show. I told him of course I am. One thing led to another, and
        then in February 2003, AJ and I kicked off *Chaz and AJ in the Morning*
        on WPLR. I had been at WPLR when Smith and Barber left the
        first time and remember the backlash encountered by the team that
        followed Smith and Barber. I expected the same kind of thing when
        Smith and Barber left again. I figured AJ and I would be the most
        hated radio show in Connecticut for a year and then it would level
        off. And then by the third year I figured we get our ratings up. But the
        backlash never really occurred, and the fans were more understanding
        this time, probably because I had a history with PLR and also the fans
        by that time figured it was already in the cards, which made it easier

for us. So for our very first ratings period, we were the number-one show, which is awesome. The second rating period came out, and we posted the highest ratings in WPLR's history, and we've done that several times since. So now we're the longest-running, highest-rated show in the history of WPLR. We have won a National Association of Broadcasters (NAB) Marconi Award for best medium market morning show, which is a crazy, crazy honor. We have been nominated for a second Marconi award and will be attending the award ceremony in New York City in October. WPLR is also nominated for Best Medium Market Rock Station.

TR   Recently, there has been a lot of discussion about artificial intelligence (AI) in many work areas. Do you think AI can replace your job as a radio disc jockey?

Chaz Well [*laughter*] I can guarantee you that we will never have any trouble being mistaken for any kind of intelligence! So, we're not worried about it. People don't tune into our show for any sort of intelligence [*laughter*], so we will certainly be okay there.

TR   How would you describe AJ?

Chaz AJ is a twelve-year-old in an older person's body. He never really got past twelve [*laughter*]. Which makes him so awesome! I've been with AJ through the most difficult periods of his life. He comes into work every day, and when that mic is on he's ready to rip and ready to do his job, which is to make people laugh. He takes great pride in that.

TR   What makes WPLR a great station?

Chaz Man, that's a great question. I would love to hear how other people, including listeners, answer that question. I think that when WPLR first came about, that was really an important time. It was a time when rock was really coming into its own and separating itself from pop music. You had Zeppelin and that music happening, and PLR became the counter-culture place to go. It was the original social media. It was the anti-establishment. I mean, when you put that WPLR sticker on your car, it meant that you were cool, it was a cool badge. I think we have been very lucky to fall into ownership that didn't mess it up. And that's very rare, there are only a few stations like this in the country now.

   I will say that WPLR has raised a ton of money for charities. I feel the most important thing a radio show can do is to be the glue of the community and help in whatever way, maybe by giving you a laugh or a chuckle in the morning on your way to work, or to bring light to an important issue, or raise money for a needy family.

TR Why is fundraising and helping the community such a big part of your show?

Chaz I remember growing up, it was a very tough time in my house with my dad not working, our home not heated properly, no phone, not a lot of food. I knew with Christmas coming up, there wouldn't be any toys. One day my dad walks in with a box of toys. Pleasantly surprised, I asked my dad, "Where did these toys come from?" He told me, "These toys are from the Salvation Army. People donate these toys for folks like us." And I always remember that moment. I never forget the feeling that somebody gets when someone in the community who they never met was thinking of them. For me, thinking back on those days, that's where the toy drive came about. We do an annual toy drive which I'm very, very proud of. We've probably raised over $2 million with our toy drives and many other activities related to toy drives and charities over the last twenty years. I'm very, very proud of giving back to the community.

TR What is your most memorable on-air moment?

Chaz To me, the most memorable moment was on a Friday, getting ready to go on vacation, when I got a text from a reporter friend of mine. She asked, "Have you heard anything about a shooting at the Sandy Hook school?" I told her that I hadn't heard anything about that situation. So I text a police friend of mine. The reply I got from him was stunning and stated, "Horrible mass casualties." This was early before anyone thought it was bad. I turned the car around and called my program director and told him I was heading in. I remember telling him, "This shooting incident was very bad." So we go back on the air and talked for days, every day, about this incident. I remember talking to Anthony, who was the assistant chief of the Sandy Hook Fire Department, who described this horrific mass shooting. On a professional level (and personal level), this was a profound moment in my career, to be on the air and have people calling in about this horrible tragedy. We had loved ones calling asking if I heard from this person or that person. I had someone calling to ask if I heard anything about a friend who was a teacher at the Sandy Hook school. The back-and-forth exchange between members of the community in the days after Sandy Hook is something I will never forget. As difficult as it was, there was no place I would rather have been.

And I think that is when radio is at its best—when radio helps the community and the people in it. There was no other outlet that could have done that but radio stations such as WPLR. And I'm proud to be in the center of that. CNN was in town covering the tragedy, heard what we were doing on the air, and sent a crew in to do a long form segment with us on how the show became the community forum.

To me, all the stunts and bits we did were all fun, but this was life-changing and, you know, was something really so important to me as to why we do radio every day. It was a career-defining moment for me.

TR   Yes, you are so right. It certainly was a life-changing moment for our entire state and even beyond Connecticut.

TR   By the way, I heard that Assistant Chief Anthony played an important moment in your life.

Chaz   Yes. He later introduced me to his cousin who I am now married to.

TR   For people who are not familiar with WPLR, how would you define the music that is played?

Chaz   Classic rock.

TR   How would you describe the role of the radio disc jockey? What is the importance of the radio disc jockey in music history?

Chaz   How many artists would we not have heard of, ever, if not for the radio disc jockey? Back in early days of WPLR, the disc jockeys would come in with an arm full of records and say, "I'm going to turn you on to this artist." A lot of these artists you would never have heard of—I mean, great artists, defining artists—that became truly successful mainly thanks to the success of the radio disc jockeys.

TR   Besides being a popular disc jockey—what other skills do you possess?

Chaz   NONE, I have really none [*laughter*]. I was just talking about that today. When I meet someone who is successful as a musician playing different instruments or a military veteran who is able to succeed in crisis situations, I think, "Man, I wish I had that." But I've been lucky with real estate so I think that would be my other life, because I'm interested in making things better than when I found them, and I love doing that with houses.

TR   How would you describe the Smith and Barber show that you replaced?

Chaz   Well, that's the morning show that put the "bricks" in morning radio at WPLR. With no disrespect to anyone who came before them, it was basically music. Smith and Barber was really PLR's very first show. WPLR is the dominant radio station, and the morning show is the dominant morning show now. But none of that was really true before Smith and Barber started doing their morning shows. I think WPLR was dominant as a rock station but as a number-one station in the market with the number-one morning show, I think Smith and Barber built that!

TR   How would you describe yourself? Your personality?

Chaz I'm probably too intense. I'm an over-thinker. I know a little bit about a lot of different subjects. I'm really interested in history; I always hated math because to me, there is no originality in math, it is what it is.

TR   What is your favorite location in the New Haven area?

Chaz My wife and I go into New Haven for its awesome food. You won't find a better pizza than the "big 4." And, when we want to go out for fine dining, we go to Encore by Goodfellas, it's a New York City dining experience right in our backyard.

TR   How would you describe your legion of listeners and fans?

Chaz We refer to our listeners as "the tribe" because we are a group of like-minded individuals who care about the community, want to laugh, want to have fun and periodically get "pissed off" about things. We describe the show as a "town hall meeting held in a frat house." Our listeners are the most generous, kind, "drop what they're doing" kind of people who truly want to help another individual or group of individuals. Our listeners are, without a doubt, the greatest group of people I have ever met or heard about in my entire career! I'm fifty-nine now and began when I was thirteen, and I have never heard of a group of people so willing to help others than the people who listen to our morning show. That is what I hope is my legacy, and that is what I'm so proud of.

TR   Chaz, I hope our readers found this interview as thoughtful and entertaining as I have.

Chaz Thank you, Tony.

Interview with AJ of the *Chaz and AJ Morning Show* on WPLR, September 14, 2023

Working with Chaz makes me do my very best. We're brothers.

TR First of all, congratulations on your awesome career!

AJ Thank you, Tony.

TR Let's start at the beginning.

TR Where were you born and raised?

AJ I was born in Huntington, Long Island, then moved to East Setauket, then Port Jefferson.

TR What city do you live in now?

AJ Milford, Connecticut.

TR What schools did you attend?

AJ Minnesauke Elementary School; Gelinas Junior High; Ward Melville High School; Suffolk Community College, Selden campus.

TR What were your favorite subjects in school—and why?

AJ English because I liked to write essays; drama, because I love to act; and choir because I like to sing.

TR What were your worst subjects in school—and why?

AJ Math. After Algebra I was lost [*laughter*]. Also, chemistry was boring, and social studies could never hold my attention.

TR Who were your favorite teachers—and why?

AJ Mr. Slick, my choral director, always inspired me to sing more, and Mr. Lozides, my drama teacher, was a huge fan of my acting abilities, in particular my comedy and improv skills.

TR When in school, did you have any on-air experience on school radio?

AJ No. My first experience was as an engineer for a college radio station.

TR Growing up, what radio stations did you listen to?

AJ WPLR, WNEW (New York) and the Long Island radio stations WBAB, WAPP and WRCN.

TR Who were your favorite disc jockeys when you were growing up?

AJ Rockin' Mike Johson, Smith and Barber, Chaz (*Camp Chaos*) and Rocky Allen (*Showgram*).

TR What was your first job after school?

AJ Stock room for Brent City Department Store.

TR What were the circumstances surrounding how you became interested becoming an on-air radio disc jockey?

AJ   I was a drum tech for a rock band, and I went with our drummer to a radio station for an on-air interview. I kept cracking one-liners, and so on the way out, I was asked by the program director if I'd ever thought of being on the air because I had a gift of gab [*laughter*]. I was hired to do middays immediately afterward.

TR   What was your first radio on-air job?

AJ   Middays at WQNR/Rock-it Radio.

TR   What were your radio jobs after that? Approximate dates?

AJ   WRCN (1990–2003), WPLR (2003–present).

TR   Recently, there has been a lot of discussion about artificial intelligence (AI) in many work areas. Do you think AI can replace radio disc jockeys (your job)?

AJ   Unfortunately, it seems to be a possibility. That would be a huge mistake because AI cannot replace genuine personality and caring.

TR   Tell me about some of your on-air stunts/skits, which were listeners' favorites?

AJ   I'd have to say the annual "Buttle Rockets" when I would shoot bottle rockets from my rear end to salute July Fourth [*laughter*]. It ran each year for twelve years.

TR   When did you first begin at WPLR?

AJ   February 2003.

TR   What was your first job at WPLR?

AJ   Same as it is now: *Chaz and AJ Morning Show* co-host.

TR   How did you meet Chaz?

AJ   I was the morning show host of WRCN. They fired me and replaced me with Chaz. I was brought back two months later to do evenings, 7:00 p.m. to 12:00 a.m.

TR   How would you describe Chaz?

AJ   Funny, driven, gets things done.

TR   What is it like working with Chaz?

AJ   Working with Chaz makes me do my best. We're brothers.

TR   What makes WPLR a great station?

AJ   It's a heritage rock station, listened to by many generations.

TR   For people who are not familiar with WPLR, how would you define the music that is played?

AJ   Classic rock.

TR   How would you describe the *Chaz and AJ Show*?

AJ   As Chaz says, it's a "town hall meeting held in a frat house."

TR   How would you describe the role of the radio disc jockey? What is the importance of the radio disc jockey in music history?

AJ   The role of a DJ is to be there when something arises and take people through their day just like a best friend would.

TR   Besides being a popular disc jockey—what other skills do you possess?

AJ   I write parody songs, I sing, I play drums, a stand-up comic and an actor in indie movies.

TR   Did you ever wish that you were a well-known musician?

AJ   I would love to be a drummer in a hard rock band.

TR   How would you describe the Smith and Barber show that you replaced?

AJ   They were legends. They helped place the "bricks" in this building. I am friends with both of them.

TR   What are your favorite bands?

AJ   The Ramones, Foghat and Kiss.

TR   How would you describe yourself?

AJ   I like to make people laugh and have a good time.

TR   What are some interesting facts about yourself?

AJ   I hate to fly, and I never had a professional pedicure.

TR   How would you describe your legions of regular listeners?

AJ   They're family. And I love to hear from family.

TR   Thank you, AJ.

AJ   My pleasure, Tony.

THE FOLLOWING IS A June 2001 interview with Ken Griffin, provided by Ed Brouder, webmaster of his outstanding WDRC site (used with permission from Ed Brouder). The year 2001 marked fifty years in radio for Ken:

Q   You spent lots of years on Hartford's airwaves. Where was home originally?

KG   I was born and raised in Waterbury, Connecticut. I started out at Waterbury's WBRY at age fourteen in 1951. I was the youngest DJ in WBRY's history.

Q   When you were a kid what people or stations did you listen to? Why did you choose radio for a career?

KG   As a kid at radio station WBRY, I got to know their afternoon drive guy, Lou Dennis, who went on to become national program director of Warner Brothers Records in Burbank, California. Alan Freed, who lived in Connecticut for a time, was also a hero. I got to work with Alan in 1959 at WINS.

Q   You were still quite young when you did press work for actor Sal Mineo. How did that come about?

KG   Sal Mineo and I were friends since 1954. I helped set up personal appearances and press for him. I also wrote articles for "teen mags" on his behalf.

Q   What were the circumstances surrounding your move from WHYN to WPOP? Were you looking or were you recruited?

KG   While at WBRY in 1960, a Mercury promo man, Hermie Dressel, became a friend. He lived in New Britain and was a former manager for Woody Herman. He liked my act at WBRY and suggested to Zack Land at WHYN that he hire me. At WHYN, I did the 10:00 a.m. to 2:00 p.m. shift plus a weekly TV dance show on Channel 40. WPOP wooed me away for better money ($200 week!) in 1964.

Q   Among your regular complement of on-air characters at WPOP were "Fats (Phats) Phontoon" and "Rocky Hill." Most listeners never realized that their lengthy dialogues were all voiced, live, by you. Tell us a little about Fats and Rocky Hill.

KG   I created Fats and Rocky to have somebody to talk to on the air. I think I had them married off at some point. They had two kids, Pebbles and Pebblina. Never could get the baby voices down, though.

Q   One of your most famous routines that you created was the Order of the Black Socks. Tell us about the Order of the Black Socks.

KG   To be honest, I can't recall what madness mentality of mine created the Order of the Black Socks. Anyway, membership cards were distributed. If you were spotted wearing black socks you won a handful of 45s from the Good Guys. Members of the Order of the Black Socks had to swear to do their best to report uncool people to "club headquarters." The routine involved distributing secret code messages to our listeners who were members or wanted to be members of the club. I'm not sure why, but it became a very popular routine. And, ironically, I heard from a member of the Hartford Symphony Orchestra recently who still carries his Order of the Black Socks card!

Q   Connecticut produced some great bands. Do you have any memories of Big Al Anderson and the Wildweeds? Or Lance Drake and the Bluebeats?

KG   I knew the very talented Al Anderson very well. After the Wildweeds, he joined another great group called NRBQ. And I discovered Lance

This certifies that

is an official member of WPOP'S

Order of the Black Socks

and is entitled to all privileges therein

Fats Fontoon, Sec'y   Ken Griffin, Big Deal

Ken Griffin's Order of the Black Socks initiation card. *Courtesy of wdrc/wpop*

Drake and The Bluebeats at a bowling alley in Brewster, New York. I got them a Columbia record deal. I lost track of Lance but heard he quit the group and joined WDRC under the name Scott Morgan.

Q   In early October 1966, you suddenly turned up in your normal shift but on a new radio station—WDRC. Why the move?

KG I made the switch to WDRC strictly for the money. Charlie Parker offered me $350 a week, $75 more than I was making at WPOP. And contrary to the popular belief by some at the time, we didn't have to wear ties and jackets. I never felt the "corporate" image at WDRC.

Q   *Scene of the Unheard* was pretty ahead of its time. Whose idea was the show, and did you choose the tunes yourself or did others have input?

KG *Scene of the Unheard* was WDRC's Bertha Porter's idea—to introduce the "new age" music. I didn't care much for it, but it seemed to work. When Charlie Parker put me in charge of the FM side and do it there, I was insulted. Like it was a step down from prestigious AM. What a schmuck I was. I remember saying to Charlie that FM would never amount to anything so I quit and went to LA, landing a p.m. shift at KGOE in Thousand Oaks and finally meeting Chuck Southcott at KGIL (a Buckley station), snagging the evening shift.

I stayed there three years, went to KIIS, then quit altogether to open my own company, American Media Systems in Newport Beach.

We ran radio schools at seven California stations, putting the students on-air at night. Great concept. I made a fortune. Also, I did voiceovers and an in-flight monthly show on TWA. I got bored in 1979, came back east to DRC, WRCQ, WMJQ (POP's FM) and WWYZ.

Q   Would you talk about some of your later ventures with Joey Reynolds in Los Angeles?

KG   Joey in L.A. Sure. He had a jingle company called Up Your Ratings in the 1970s. I worked with him on that and liaison with Drake-Chenault stations, including KHJ. Basically, we partied all the time but got to be friends with a lot of the Hollywood "elite." Can I drop a few names? Dick Clark, Ed McMahon, Rod Roddy, Frank Slay, George Carlin, Jerry Bishop, Wink Martindale, Gary Owens, etc. That's enough.

Q   Who were the really fun guys to work with?

KG   Who was fun to work with? All of the aforementioned guys. I especially miss Lou Terri, Sal LaRosa, John Sherman and Tom Shovan, who have died.

Pretty soon you and me will be the only ones left! Thanks for the memory trip you took me on. I'm writing *The Radio Chronicles: (50 Years of Broadcasting Zaniness)*, which will probably be finished on my death bed. Stay in touch.

BIBLIOGRAPHY

Personal Communications

AJ. Interview and personal communications with author, September 14, 2023

Anderson, Al. Personal communications, email and phone correspondence with author.

Arnell, Ginny. Personal communications, email and phone correspondence with author.

Brouder, Ed. Personal communications and email correspondence with author.

Cavaliere, Felix. Personal communications, email and phone correspondence with author.

Chaz. Interview and personal communications with author, September 14, 2023

Crean, Paula Renzoni. Personal communications, email and phone correspondence with author.

Dunaway, Dennis. Personal communications, email and phone correspondence with author.

Evans, Chris. Personal communications, email and phone correspondence with author.

Evans, Ken. Personal communications, email and phone correspondence with author.

Ferrante, Al. Personal communications, email and phone correspondence with author.

Freed, Judith Fisher. Personal communications, email and phone correspondence with author.

Ganter, Marty. Personal communications, email and phone correspondence with author.

Gee, Ashley. Personal communications and email correspondence with author.

Greene, Mike. Personal communications and email correspondence with author.

Kalt, Dick. Personal communications, email and phone correspondence with author.

Koob, Bill. Personal communications, email and phone correspondence with author.

Lyons, Danny. Interview and personal communications with author, August 25, 2023

Morra, Marty. Personal communications, email and phone correspondence with author.

Ohlman, Christine. Personal communications, email and phone correspondence with author.

Pacelli, Paul. Personal communications, email and phone correspondence with author.

Paiva, Bob. Personal communications, email and phone correspondence with author.

Parker, Steve. Personal communications, email and phone correspondence with author.

Parris, Fred and Emma. Personal communications, email and phone correspondence with author.

Philamonjaro. Personal communications, email and phone correspondence with author.

Potter, Jeff. Personal communications, email and phone correspondence with author.

Robinson, Dick. Personal communications, email and phone correspondence with author.

Rosenay, Charles. Personal communications, email and phone correspondence with author.

Rybak, Stefan. Personal communications, email and phone correspondence with author.

Smith, Brian. Interview and personal communications with author September 14, 2023.

Stephens, Bill. Personal communications, email and phone correspondence with author.

Warren, Al. Personal communications and email correspondence with author.

Win, Marcia. Personal communications, email and phone correspondence with author.

Wolt, Ken. Personal communications, email and phone correspondence with author.

Yutenkas, Dorothy. Personal communications, email and phone correspondence with author.

Websites

Chaz and AJ | chazandaj.com

Christine Ohlman | christineohlman.net, reverbnation.com/christineohlman

ctpost | ctpost.com

Dennis Dunaway | dennisdunaway.com

Felix Cavaliere | felixcavalieremusic.com

Fifth Estate Band | thefifthestateband.com

Legends Radio | legendsradio.com

Liverpool Productions Entertainment | liverpoolproductions.com

99.1 PLR | wplr.com

Philamonjaro | philamonjaro.com

Setlist Wiki | setlist.fm

Society for the Preservation of the Great American Songboook | preserveourgas.org

The Trick Is to Keep Going | thetrickismusic.com

WDRCOBG | wdrcobg.com

WeBe108 | webe108.com

WICC | wicc600.com

WOW Radio | io.securenetsystems.net/cwa/WOW

INDEX

ABOUT THE AUTHOR

Tony Renzoni is the author of the well-received books *Connecticut Rock 'n' Roll: A History*; *Connecticut Softball Legend Joan Joyce*; *Connecticut Bootlegger Queen Nellie Green*; *Historic Connecticut Music Venues: From the Coliseum to the Shaboo*; *Connecticut's Girls of Summer: The Brakettes and the Falcons*; *Joan Joyce: The Wonder Girl*, and *Rock 'n' Roll Connecticut: Magic Moments and Unforgettable Disc Jockeys*.

Tony had a thirty-eight-year career with the federal government. As district manager in Connecticut's Fairfield County, he oversaw the operations of four field offices, serving over 100,000 beneficiaries. He wrote over one thousand weekly columns that were published in the *Connecticut Post* newspaper and on the paper's website. Tony was a recipient of more than forty awards, including his agency's highest honor award.

A lifelong resident of Connecticut, Tony is a graduate of Sacred Heart High School in Waterbury and Sacred Heart University in Fairfield.

Tony Renzoni serves as a consultant for the hit play *Joan Joyce! Musical*, which is based on his book *Connecticut Softball Legend Joan Joyce*.

Books by Tony Renzoni

Connecticut Rock 'n' Roll: A History
Connecticut Softball Legend Joan Joyce
Connecticut Bootlegger Queen Nellie Green
Historic Connecticut Music Venues: From the Coliseum to the Shaboo
Connecticut's Girls of Summer: The Brakettes and The Falcons
Joan Joyce: The Wonder Girl
Rock 'n' Roll Connecticut: Magic Moments and Unforgettable Disc Jockeys